WEAK LINK

Rob Halpern

a t e l o s

42

ISBN: 978-1-891190-42-1

First edition, first printing

Atelos

A Project of Hip's Road
Editors: Lyn Hejinian & Travis Ortiz
Text and Cover Design and Typesetting: Derek Fenner
Cover Image: Dee Dee Kramer from "Corrugated Love Poem 16: Being Seen" (2013)

Contents

Hoax
9

Harnessed
19

Theses on the Remembrance of Things to Come (28-48)
65

The Rhetoric of Blood
75

Pornotopias
85

Weak Link
119

Of Bodies and Waste
149

The Wound and the Camp, or Visceral Solidarity
165

My Augustine (A Fragment)
189

Acknowledgments
197

HOAX

— behold the body —

Not too long ago, I was turned-on to a curious little nineteenth-century volume attributed to one William Swinton called *Rambles Among Words* (1861). It's a compendium of folk etymologies whose aim is to rehearse the roots and rhizomes of a specifically American idiomatic English in relation to its Anglo-Saxon past, and it's suspected that Walt Whitman had a strong hand as Swinton's ghost-collaborator. Eschewing scholarly philology, *Rambles Among Words* opts instead for the pleasures of anecdote and hearsay. Often, I'll open this book casually and randomly, as one might do with the *I-Ching*, seeking a word or phrase to guide me thru the day. One morning, I opened to the entry "Hocus-Pocus" and was astonished to read:

> 'Hocus-pocus' is said to be a monkish muddle for 'Hoc est corpus' (the formula, 'Here is the body [of Christ],' etc.), a corruption of fantastic origin. And if it be true that the ignorant and juggling priests who gabble Latin which they do not understand, instead of saying 'Hoc est corpus' transformed it into 'hocus-pocus,' may we not legitimately form the word 'hoax' from this?

So the hoax of meaning arrives homophonically as language moves in the space between "hoc est corpus"—*behold the body*—and "hocus-pocus"—*watch it disappear*.

Take Gerhard Richter's *Decke* (1988) as an illustration of what will never be illustrated here. Translated in English as "Blanket," Richter's work first renders and then conceals an iconic photograph of Gudrun Ensslin's hanged body in a prison cell, an image that circulated widely in the German press after the alleged suicide of the prominent Red Army Faction (RAF) radical in 1977. Strung-out between abstract dematerialization and post-minimalist figuration, *Decke* absorbs the photograph and then disfigures its referent. Working over its own rendered image corrosively, Richter's paint becomes a cover, a screen, a veil. Whereas the photograph's forensic conceit lies in its appeal to visual proof that the disputed event had indeed taken place (as if the body itself were thereby able to speak its truth), Richter negates the photo's presumed self-evidence—he even negates his own painting's seizure of its mediatized image—and as everyone knew, the event itself could easily have been staged to cover-up a state-sanctioned murder, a good bit of fake news, as it were.

I saw Richter's *Decke* at the Palazzo Strozzi in Florence in the spring of 2010 as part of an exhibition entitled "Gerhard Richter and the Disappearance of the Image," which situated Richter's paintings beside those of seven other contemporary artists, but I was only riveted by this one work. My friends abandoned me to the gallery as I lingered there, straining to see what isn't there to see. As my body inclined toward the canvas, I thought I could detect the recessed lines of a door frame whose muted gray tones become visible and white, while the fullness of Ensslin's hanging body remains almost completely erased, leaving nothing but the faintest trace in the upper middle of the painting, as a chaotic pattern—all static and noise—eats away at the rest, and an etched grid emerges to replace a spectral vision. This is how the past irrupts in a present that isn't present to see. Under the painter's brush, the event—Ensslin's alleged suicide—withdraws in the corrosion of image, both having become submerged in haze as a sheet of paint covers the figure the way a blanket or a shroud would cover the body.

I am writing this essay years after my only encounter with Richter's *Decke*, and given that the painting has only been infrequently cataloged, I've often had to consult online images in an effort to reconstruct my vision, so who knows what I really saw. While I can recreate the movement of rooms across the gallery, and the placement of works on its walls, I really don't know what I was seeing upon seeing Richter's painting even as I imagine the feeling of its singular detail or punctum—the recessed lines of a door, the sole remaining trace of referential meaning—as though it were lodged inside my body somewhere between bladder and liver, a muted hum or shiver. But this is pure retrospection, a kind of necromancy. Here's what I remember with the clarity of ice: As I stand in the gallery, I can feel myself longing for my friends to realize they had lost me, as all the energy of my thoughts and affections organize themselves like a spell to draw them back, to see me captured by this thing and wonder why.

The scandal of Richter's fifteen paintings re-presenting the controversy around the RAF—a unified collection of works titled *October 18, 1977*—has been well-rehearsed, and while this sequence is in some respects beside my point, it's worth noting that all the paintings in this collection bear literal titles like *Cell, Hanged, Funeral, Record Player*, and *Dead.* I knew nothing of these paintings when, at the Palazzo Strozzi, I fell upon Richter's *Decke*—or, *Blanket*—which was *not* included in the cycle of works that first showed in Cologne in the winter of 1989 as it's one of his discarded renderings of Ensslin's hanged body that he later painted over. Separated from the original sequence, *Decke* remains the cycle's appendix, its afterthought, its commentary, its codicil. It's also an outcast, a secret, a runt. In contrast to its privileged litter, *Decke* alone bears a title that is at once metaphorical, self-referential and excessive in its connotation.

From the vantage point of its composition, ten years after the events it recalls, Richter's painting arouses a ghost, a specter of state violence and obstructed mourning, be it for the idea of a German nation or its revolutionary transformation. But the thing aroused is only ever a cover or a screen, indeed, a *Decke*, which could denote a bedspread, rug or quilt, while connoting concealment, protection, refuge, or even disguise, with figurative expressions like *unter die Decke kriechen*, to pull the covers over one's head, to protect oneself by hiding, as if under a blanket. Then there is *zudecken* (to put a blanket on something or someone), *bedecken* (to cover something, like your body), and *verdecken* (to mask, disguise or conceal). At the same time, *Decke* denotes a ceiling or roof, a structural limit, which also suggests the painting's frame, allowing some things to enter the picture while keeping other things out. There are expressions like *es tropft von der Decke* (there's water coming through the ceiling) and even *von der Decke hängen* (to hang from the ceiling). As the figural and the literal converge, pivot, and invert, Richter's pun achieves an extraordinary richness. My German friend Christian offered the *coup de grace* when he confirmed in an email from Frankfurt: "And when the police ask you about a suspect and you say that you don't know this person or that you won't say anything about them—this is *jemanden decken.* And *verdeckt* means 'undercover,' you know, like an agent." Significantly, too, there's the expression *mit jemandem unter einer Decke stecken* (to be in bed with), suggesting a kind of complicity—Richter's? the viewer's?—which is something the painter seems to be concerned about a great deal, especially in *October 18, 1977*, and in the case of this painting the question is unavoidable.

Returning then to this cover-up called *Decke*, I remember perceiving the vague hint of a linen sash with which Ensslin's body hangs in Richter's rendering of its photographic image—or maybe I just want to see this now—and while noting the way he covers this image twice, first in the sense of "covering" a pop song, and then by throwing a cover over the cover (covering himself like in a gesture of shame?), I can still feel my gaze pushing up against the frame as if, were the ceiling only higher, the strain of seeing nothing might be relieved.

Richter's approach to the politics of representation feels a bit like Warhol's inverse and complement: Not a commercial image whose saturation in the public sphere of privatized communication is tantamount to the mystification of its referent—be it a celebrity like Marilyn or a commodity like Brillo—but rather a mystified image whose saturation in the social imaginary covers up its referent—by which I do *not* mean in this instance Ensslin's body, but rather the

State. Maybe *Decke* formalizes the way the omnipresence of state violence is withdrawn inside every spectacular image wherein that violence becomes ungraspable, obscured, shrouded, taboo to even speak of it. I can't help but wonder now whether the hygienic erasure of violence from discourse—by which I *do* mean the way forms of historical and structural violence often become unspeakable—conditions the delusion of a peaceful public sphere whose policing function can then assume its license undercover.

When first speaking to my friends of my initial impressions of Richter's *Decke*, my tongue slips on the name "Ensslin" and falls on that of "Esenin"—as in Sergey Esenin—the popular Soviet poet who, at age 30 in 1925, took his own life, leaving behind a final "Farewell Poem," written in the poet's own blood, which concludes with the couplet: "In this life to die is nothing new / But to live, of course, is nothing newer." Esenin's romantic farewell was the occasion for Vladimir Mayakovsky's poem, "To Sergey Esenin" (1926), a critical riposte that condemns Esenin's sentimental attachment to suicidal sadness and its pathetic expression in bad verse: "Why make / the number / of suicides more?" While Mayakovsky's poem seems to suggest that people might kill themselves because Esenin's poem is truly awful, his larger meaning concerns the fact that Esenin's bad verses actually moved people to suicide as an imaginary way to transcend social suffering by avoiding any real confrontation with its conditions.

Esenin's poem is forensic, not because it is written in the poet's own blood—the literalization of a romantic cliché—but because it organizes social knowledge that won't reduce to private meaning. But while forensic evidence as a form of public testimony wants to preserve the documentary ruse of its purity and neutrality, it nevertheless betrays an intense subjectivity, a pathos of integrity, a falsely immediate meaning, just as personal emotion is always vulnerable to the social forces that put it to work. How can Esenin's words—"Goodbye my friend you live in my heart"—be anything but clear and simple? If history is what really hurts, how can an expression of historical suffering be true and false at the same time? Mayakovsky's ruthless rejoinder opens a space of contestation over the significance of that forensic information. This is the argument in *How are Verses Made?*, Mayakovsky's book-length essay on poetry as a social good that uses "To Sergey Esenin" as its primary illustration: For a poem to be worth its salt, it must respond to real exigency—a political imperative, or "social command" as Mayakovsky calls it—in order to create a counter-fact that challenges the force of "common sense." And one of the exigencies to which Mayakovsky's poem responds is the urgent need to stem the rising tide of suicidal despair fueled by bad poetry.

In fucking with the forensic narrative surrounding Esenin's death—lifting, mocking and turning its phrases, i.e., "In this life / to die / has never been hard. // To make new life / 's more difficult / by far."—I like to think that Mayakovsky's poem anticipates Richter's *Decke*, the way it wrests something seemingly evidentiary away from a repressive apparatus of meaning-making. For a more recent illustration of what I think of as a counter-forensic aesthetic practice, one might think of Claudia Rankine's manner of fucking with the iconic image of a lynching in *Citizen*.* Rather than paint over a painted representation of a photographed "suicide" as Richter does, or write over the bloody lines of a poem as Mayakovsky does, Rankine erases the image of a black body hanging from a tree, thereby turning attention instead on the social agents of that violence—bemused white bodies acting with impunity—rather than its spectacular effect. If all three of these works expose anything at all, perhaps it is how aesthetic codes confuse or conflate exposure and concealment, testimony and censorship, document and repression.

* I've adopted the concept of "counter-forensics" from Allan Sekula's "Photography and the Limits of National Identity" (1993): "Counter forensics, the exhumation and identification of the anonymised ('disappeared') bodies of the oppressor state's victims, becomes the key to a process of political resistance and mourning." Quoted in Thomas Keenan, "Counter-forensics and Photography," *Grey Room* 55 (Spring 2014).

Just as the RAF reminded its German public that whatever economic well-being West Germany may have achieved by the 1970s was haunted by a historical violence it could no longer perceive, or preferred not to, Richter's canvas uncannily materializes the very fiber of a social imagination whose abstractions had become the concrete material of everyday life. *Decke*'s gauzy screen is painted over a painting of a popular image ten years after its dissemination, and this is no mere minimalist trope, but the figure of what is paradoxically most present and whose documents have become profoundly abstract. In other words: Richter simultaneously materializes the persistence of the past in the present and the absence of the present in the representation of that past.

Decke contains a social wound where the false immediacy of communication has been interrupted as one's sense of that immediacy becomes a keenly felt effect of its mediated decomposition. Richter paints the erosion of cultural memory on the very images that constitute it. In doing so, he becomes a kind of realist as the dissolution of history becomes visible in the very images that represent that history. One might say that the so-called "Event" is the image that displaces the historical fact by becoming it. In Richter's painting, the withdrawal of the referent—be it history, state, or police—opens a void [——] where the viewer's sensorium feels strangely replete with the eroding sensation of what it can't perceive. Still, a rhetoric of this image circulates through its withdrawal, in whose place emerges that void—let's call it "the public sphere," or merely its placeholder—where one can only express oneself clearly in bad faith.

In short, Richter's *Decke* presents the viewer with the exquisite image of a social mirage—an allegory of the photograph's absent content—and this becomes the painting's substance. As the manifestation of a sanctioned cover-up that doubles as an inchoate national fantasy, *Decke* materializes the bad faith of good conscience while making legible a whole aesthetics of the public secret: the referent being a highly publicized hoax—*behold the body!*—whose representation neutralizes further investigation into its conditions of possibility. As if to say "This has nothing to do with that fakery!," or, "Look closely and you'll see the thing defrocked!," the painting allegorizes the procedure of the cover—*Decke*—like a kind of make-over, a reenactment or revision behind which there is nothing more to see, the secret of the hoax being that there is no secret.

HARNESSED

— what claims our ravaged bodies
from consuming dark —

LOVERS OF KAIROS

And having not remembered all this at all nor where we will
Have sung again or tread in place of nothing having taken place
But the place itself arrives not perceiving the shots

An imperceptible slough the screen a landscape drags
Generic no-shows more than notion's nothing's pure to call
This thing a common place names no meaning others call

A body a war closed futures whose boundaries bind my trade
A trope for what's not here I traffic in imponderables motes
Organs jerk whose use you are my biohazard my dump.

PRELUDE TO COMMODIOUS

This is where it gets pretty personal hemmed in
- side acts enclosing sense eroding all my needs
For warmth & honey common phantoms things

Sing of use not being on our side they press again
- st my limit being a swarm becoming corralled
Inside the same nonsite falling to a cop's baton

Not failing the place property erases you see for
- ce shifting lines converging undoing time
The way we make it deep how deep the ground

Dreaming futures not being bound to rates rent
Open squares under private siege a coup
Like common sense undone the library itself hi

- jacked commanded dumped by armed pretenders
Say the commode goes up in smoke say what
You are has been revoked utopian imaginary

Say whatever you want has been unmade
& ready to be made again with
- drawn people arouse

— *the place itself, this hole in the goods.*

AN ESSAY ON THE SIEGE

The barricades were far away when the sinew of system's rule
Pit me up against my friend whose politics I'd suspected
But managed to avoid until the bombs began to fall. Ruined
Aftermath of monument, lodged deep in throat, the cubicle
Enclosed my tongue-splayed spectacle as it lay bare, or bare
- ly consonant with itself while the alphabet, aroused & unwieldy
Expands the limit's extremity, the law now incarnate in the PD
- 's baton & shielded horizon where our bodies press the gown
A forced caress. So absolute a distance haunts this proximate
Closeness turning my feelings into gas, a sublime state. Or maybe
It's the other way around seeing how my GPS app tells me there's
Someone closer to my own location than myself. Our convers
- ation was void from the start, cunningly masked as common
Sense whose unfailing power the situation so perfects or perfect
- ly harnesses, the way the war has harnessed its own image and
Disfigures my voice inside each contemporary object, the poem

Where inaudible logics of death & expansion find hospitable
Repose. Whatever autonomy my writing falsely promises liquid
- ates in endless yearning, sweet sentiment of the dying world
I keep hearing about, dreaming of everyone I love turned back
At the line between 'free zone' and 'siege' like the tour guide said
In Sarajevo where unaligned forces once called for appeasement.
But that was long ago under Clinton when state sponsored human
- itarian aid was better prepared to mask the moneyed squeeze.
Would that I were only able to take revenge on my dumb interior
Whose squeezed interests here join strategic targets there, securing
My self or at least its image to a state of nature. That's a theory
Of personhood I guess. So I close my eyes and summon pictures
Of his body, getting off on these sad feelings. Bombs were falling
Already on [——] in accord with figures of justice whose

Congruity with public opinion produces plosive torsions
My syntax, unconvincing, the embarrassing tics, a social stutter
Masked by product or its negation as my skin breaks out in fabled
Currencies undermining each position, these zones of tacit agree
- ment, a whole archipelago of reason's debris dissembling more
Familiar forms of speech or a blank in the world system where
Every cry reduces to the known & measured, so dismissed.
Common places erode as quickly as they harden around
Disguised command, whatever promises to bring me pleasure
The ruin of money itself against whose pricing surface my poem
Assumes a form of emergency management, clinging to its private
Effects. Boys garnish dreamy signs withdrawn from use, the wound
Itself an index of event, this vacuole, my error, a gurney where the
Body lies. It's still unclear what meaning the poem conducts, how
One thing fattens as another lies prone for feeding. Just tell me
What square to be at now that all my friends are gone, like every

- one's sleeping off defeat whose premonitions haunt my gestures
In advance to parry the coming blow or at least not give in to it
- 's dumb nature. Okay, the poem might fake a feeling or cop a feel
From which it turns to blush as familiar moves & vulgar meanings
Pool in excess of what makes my movements sing. I have a song
About his hair I'm anxious to sing for you, but it'll have to wait. Yes
Carnage over there relates to obesity here, but this eludes my analysis
The way a detainee's own study in hunger hangs upon my fable
- d meat. Between equal rights, force decides the way it always has
But my tongue, still splayed, makes me incomprehensible, a needle
In a dusty groove, his body coming back in a shipping box again
And again, tracing the routes of all my agile products from forest
And factory hewn as they measure my body's place and coin
- cide with the park, a riot in color & light, auratic haze, his belly
Riddled with holes, my pillow. A soldier's piss, warm broth in my
Throat, a sweet digestif after horror & debt, wherever I can have his
Fire being where I'll have it. This is how I give myself away, naked

Before the other, a risk adjusted exposure conned by branded terms
Joining spirit & bone, commonplaces I name myself the way a blank
Floats thru my verse, patient sinew of that spasm, becoming song
The one I mentioned, being of his hair, I haven't forgotten it
His gentle fat whereupon I love to sleep, there being no reasonable
Utterance, no hope in speech without excluding someone I might want
To persuade, like you, or naming myself as one persuaded as if I could
Name anything true about my own condition whose appearance fails
The poem's perception. Being a hazy form of apprehension, my half
Awakened sentence can't bear witness to impossible voids [——]
Where the bombs keep falling and cries never cease. But even this
Arousal sings the failure of rational distribution as fantasy engulfs
My form being impress of that absence, ruse of my wellbeing. Some

- one said the future lives lodged in the present's contradictions
Another vanishing moment disappearing inside movements of debt
Whose consciousness I find myself regaining on the toilet
Of a transatlantic flight, desperate for a form to help me manage
My feelings, conditions having rendered my friendship otherwise
Impossible. In a world that wants to subsume every side, the poem
Has to take a side. I gotta say I'm astonished to be writing to you
Without experiencing my incontinence as an effect of lousy
Planning, imprudent investment recalling the way I once had
To empty my bowels before entering that sex club at 1808 Market
With nowhere to go before paying the fee. But that was long ago
Before the city changed and my friends began fucking online.
Arguments like these merely function to affirm the most
Depressing triumphs of common sense confirming things
Already here, all our digits having become obscure prostheses
Of militarized event, vehicles of tinted flight before which I
Lurch from occurrence to occurrence, desperately
Making all these stupid calls

— *to the dead in whom this dream will not come true.*

THE USUFRUCT OF THE LAND
(BEING NO SOLUTION TO CRISIS)

•

No poems accumulate
What use fusts in us un
- used wealth a hole a

Field the so-called free
- farmer's plasm buys the
Body back or sells the ba

- by for a share what large
Seigniorial domains and
All you want is waste

- ed arable earth my fat
Makes up the difference
In cash so ashamed I have

— *used the usufruct for shitting.*

•

Hurled on the market
A *fosse commune* what
Movements hulk away

My bowels' landed weal
- th a whole decay of
People upon whom

Care encroaches ten
- ants singing shit & all
That grows ploughs

Depopulates erects
These beautiful lines
Enclosures to enjoy

— *a thing is to use it illicitly.*

•

What a common grave or
Blank for this I have so
Been fucked into pasture

Pleasures the sovereign
- 's length a rent-roll my
Lordship my bondsman

For whom I'd give it all

— *his hole can't justify my longing.*

•

Pauper ubique jacet ex
- clama la reina Isabel
Después de recorrer

Inglaterra upon seeing
Things limping *en masse*
To the capital cast off mist

- resses of my surplus
Value clings in barely
Living limbs bowels vow

Be buried near my hinter
Lands glittering zombies
Appear from the treasury

- 's crapulous surfaces
Stones now mourn

— this common resource.

•

Now to possess what po
- ssesses us a fusting
Possession of every use

Glittering in *shmaltz* be
- coming *schmerz* feeding
What hungers won't

Die for forcible means
Employed from sheep
- walks to cities tracing files

Crossing pirouettes tra
- verse enclosures forcing
A zero degree an endless

Consumption devours
Things already so devou
- red mulched in a pretty

Sweet parody of a soldier
- 's mimetic energy

— *whoa so inexhaustible.*

•

This identity has no organs it
Can die without any body
Dying an eggshell a skin my

Slave morality being landed
Gentry laws of settlement in
- demnify these instated limbs

No organs know what to use

— *a thing is not to use it.*

•

Say direct seizure *haute*
Finance arouses the dead
Like my need for credit

Contracts a name a multi
- tude of situations a crisis
Seeming communal im

- posthume *munis* in latin
Means *gift* 'immunity' be
- ing the gift's refusal so

We've refused & organized
Our refusal to go down
Amping up the logic what

A horror I've become
The nation's good taste
For bodies so shorn of

Names historically ex
- posed to force no tree
I being every one of them

— *things sheep are driven from.*

•

Feel my thing slipping in
- to unspeakable pleas
- ure this shit equals com

- munal leveling practice
Breeding distinction the
Way yr credit hole honors

Dishonorable stink holes
Sustaining accumulation
So dispossessing dis

- emboweling debou
- ching already drained so
- ldiers can fuck me can't

Relieve my bowels
Whose body's no bound
- aries die of all we are

Dying from doing this
Being common waste

— *wild beasts the birds.*

BIRD CRAVE

No license to refuse this love whose names call out from the hooded hole
My face in you becomes so near a distance where clarity's all blasted i
- sotopic quavering a fazing eros yr conceptual remains beyond this blind
Bird of consequence a concrete drift obscures the light we see by
Ourselves being no light at all a fall

- ing out of light even as yr eyes disjoin
My selves abstract inconstant rates inflate the sun could be
A turbine a stone bone moss birds crave conversion too inside the fault
My poem runs to silence slows these things

Become us truer names than ours we
Can't hear any more

— *this waste thru which our matter rises.*

ENTHYMEME

Bunker busters heat my home and plenty
- 's holes void dreams to drain this mother
Of all the harnessed & the fucked we are

Of the same force fingers pumping cotton
- fierce an instinct or some vague collective
Zeal harnessed cells drains fetters his being

Empty linen drapes security being equal
To detained here I am of the things they use
To stuff dirty men in what has not occurred

Or the force with which it blows I am of them
Feeling something spreading out of things
Thwarts fingers my impotence sorrow comes

In waves wars like this one being but a mass
- ive grave of signs so desperate to refer seek
Refuge in cells as if to force what all this me

- ans sounds floating blanks be real a drain
No ratio measures my cargo of man

— *gled bones.*

LOCAL FINISH

Swallow foul the soul suck filth
- y sun resource and watch me
Come inside this mini tank regime

The poem allows you to report
On my own late nite emissions
Trading methane straight carbon

Airs & muniments conspiring a
Kinder love laid over this kind
Of labor it's useless being held in

- side free base feelings like these
Drown in piss slakes makes me sing
Joining hands at choke points

Arousing revenge on my interior all
The odors the house & garden cling
- ing to sounds exceeding my lame i

- deas I mean the moneyed décor
Licking a soldier's nippies blown
Flesh stinks & stools whose pink

I can even get off on my own
Trace particles and coins

— rent my body this way so you don't have to.

•

Let's say we've acquired
A function just by speaking
Of what approximates one

Organ being of sound the
Mind falls into anything can
Be money if it's the only

Thing one makes ok the ear
- rth I mean the earth is
The only thing I can't hear

A thing you can't even see
But for the freight the body
Being sheer see-thru veneer

Relations no longer attract
Lacking sound these sounds
For things I still can't feel.

•

Whatever you want to put inside
Me there I can always swallow
More is a little like saying I can

Lend obscurity right out of my
Self seeking sovereignty there
On his belly not imagining any

- thing freer than the pleasure good
Society harbors faint contusions ill
- umine fractured scapula dark raised

Midline abdominal lesions reveal anti
- cubital fossa getting off on the parts
Barren reports prosthetic fingers

Inside take revenge on my fucking
Car its interior environs harden dark
Tissue hemorrhaging fake blood

Swelling things I'd rather put inside
Where all the odors no longer
Smell of powder even ammo equals

Money being true décor being no
Real day despite the sun his swollen
Balls my little coo-coo nuts be

- long to the base sucking clusters
Tender strokes against yr harms.

•

Not functioning all this ap
- proximates money attracting
Things unskilled meaning labor

Or the day laborer I love
From a distance my car pro
- tects his value his thighs attract

The state's pure noise fun
- ctioning like the mind
Stands in for what falls out

Of all relation the body balks
Account as organs fail no
One really is the economic

Thing being a question of onto
- logy always sneaking back
Inside my snatch.

•

Common meat remains aroused
A thin dark layer a hyoid bone
A vitreous fluid obscure tissue

Sourced out my holes & stuffed
W/ signs of things displace
Exchange rates diminishing an

- gled toward the faint commode
A contract fades behind the eyes
Won't close what rubber feeds

Clots fattens limbs confuse these
Parts exceed whose phone fucks
Deep in bone booms shingles play

Far flung his genitals blown right
Off the base frees what the grid
Grafts futures extracting value

The honeyed hole my bowels
So clean the skin can't sing this.

•

No body being common cause
Can sing diminished wipes ruins
Worlds lubed toys IEDs wires

Limbs dispatching lumps elect
- ric parts freezing bones fake
Bloodied hole way down clean

Where we'll go & share a single
Lung in some dumb motel
For the good life means

Work harder stitch for less
Futures grafting severed meat
To stumps pawn the gen intel

Whose salvage selving coins
Stashing worlds to hang on
Words like sky

— *say thin locale.*

CALLING SWEET ALL NOXIOUS SIMPLES

These lines can mime the thing no longer
W/ my arms voiding peoples & the sun
Rising in the East it all remains a blank
Somewhere in China whose money remains
A mystery the very thing I need to sing
I need yr mouth inside me for any sound
To sound alone inside my youth & my
Finance escaping w/ yr hands going deep
Deep inside inflexible senses sensing so
Many occlusions of sense like yr cock that
Means nothing but an absence in public

Works projects or whatever makes living
Fun when it's all been abstracted flushed
Wasted like yr name's become insoluble
As a contract & a lot of ranting my rants
Having forgotten the dead having given
Up on us not watching or only watching
The circuitry the vessels tangled in ravish
- ing sounds like a government busting up
The caps & trade getting off in my hand

— *these visions of shadow futurity.*

HOW TO LIBERATE YR BODY FROM SOCIAL NECESSITY
after Martha Rosler

Ha ido usted al mercado? yup, 'estregue' means 'scrub' the dome
- stic foundation of every house where the bodies don't
Wash up here and everyone's entitled to a beautiful interior

— *so aroused by my birthright.*

ROCK SONG

Being nothing seen this rock no place no
Eye to follow things erase this common
Hole in sense sinks cleaves things scales can't
Sense insensate force what's living here and
Dying not to die breathing things produce
This rock no point to vanish splits no bird
Can name what's got no name and shudders
In this fateless space no nominal blow no
Relation in relation no history tho in history
Lost not seeing nothing but the fateful force

By which nothing can't be named it names
Things useless the question being use itself
A unit of measure in the economic organ
- ization of dreamboats whose raptures de
- scribe what nothing resembles this feels like
Rock a place no site can split screens birds fly
Motionless cresting zones points things name
No event the distance jets one bird from sky
A thrush beyond this loss to lose what goes

— *withdrawn into the square.*

THIS CELL IN MY HEAD, BEING MADE OF WAX

Don't talk of 'stages' cause I'm fucking co
- ld and frozen forms can't express the real
Force police equivalence development ground
Rent makes our mirrors the effects of more
Uneven tyrannies than the one they staged
Under other skies long ago spells no more
Than words I've said when the talk gets real

- ly monstrous more than what we love we do
In yr country I mean yr person where the object
Form of things becomes another self-reference
To the auto I rent accruing industrious glamour
That's not ours to hold in you I've held some
- thing fashioning skin no bone remains a pool
Casts back yr image where no reflection waits
For me the calcified and hollowed sign my
Sleep's become until now unnamed as vision

When there's nothing more to see I think I've
Seen thru fog to a dark of such pitch the screen
Goes white with it so much light calls an end
To stages because things can't go on deve
- loping anymore resistance to regime
Being what one sees when one be
- lieves irrupts inside this hole
In what we sense

— *I mean yr body in a tent, the sky.*

HOW TO THINK 'COMMONS' WITH NO RECOURSE TO RIGHTS

As anarch blunders
Shibboleths cling to du
- mb tongues like mine
Betraying selves nations

Dead conditions signs
The sentence being a
- cousmatic subspace
Haunting nothing no

Ear comes to comfort
Me the words move
My body goes audio a
Transit scene an impact

Say the only thing literal
Death encloses currents
The way exchange fun
- ctions like no land

Functions as land sky
Being no sky no sea
Floats streams move
Calving low lying ice

Floes the air preserves
The talk & salt leaches
Into leverage or shells
Stone to bone here lies

‘Here lies’

— *all clove asunder.*

LITERAL HALLUCINATION

Plugging holes my poems do nothing
Real but fake value these events having not
Occurred as the bottom presses into fiber
- less memory from which I'll never recover
Myself a heap the words hallucinate & blow
Me from top down singing *I love big valves*
Meaning every dumb poem plugs fish &
Shrimp descending sky gently landing
On skin things peacefully die into image

A withdrawn photo fondly fakes the poem
Coming up from below *just shut it off* I sing
In my dream of the pipe and it closes like
Some *fond du commerce* being always false
Bottom ready to vanish as subsea source
Allows things to gush but this isn't real
- ly what happens is you give me big blow
- out preventers and shoot epoxy up
My fucking hole *I'm no top* I say so I don't

Protest there being no witness no role
To fake the body itself a cenotaph
Whose remains remain elsewhere intimate
W/ my fluids & finance the self being equal
To a wellbore structure compromised
Further down hole like the poem being
Nature's fulfillment my bona fide fake
Protector sleek plume drain try the junk
Shot crotch shot fails the goods kill

W/ barrels of heavy soil mud to stop
Crude in 3 attempts at rates of up to
80 barrels a minute dirt & concrete recall
- ing pit sand & river sand funds deploy
Relief empty formalisms whiteners dis
- persants can't overcome the company or
- gans wedged safety subsea ruptures infra
- structure during surge the gas being mine
Own sensation a bubble opening deep

Inside the poem encloses things free
- ly escaping into ether when it's all made
Of fiber my special protective covering me
- lts to skin made of the same processes
As things pressure flows becoming lack
Of fund raising events bulk 450 tons one
Cargo bodies buried in layers of sea floor
Reports commercial fondue shrimp car
- casses of trade gulf silt fossils vanishing

Bottoms I'm not meant to be one holding
Subseas in my fluid can't even feel myself
Singing the poem fakes value contracts
Tightening the caps literally hallucinating
The hole never having to touch the floor
No singing can sing

— *how feeble fond things weaken blow.*

BELOW MEANS PROPERTY'S GOTTA END SOMEWHERE

Wherever yr dead labor washes bodies up into my forgotten gutters
Zones these holes now occupied blank estates open
Caesuras fake lots inside the *vena cava* I can spell it yr name I can
Even scream the thing because there's no one

I mean there's no jubilation
In the body per se only a bunch of musical equivalents for love
Going *la la la* eternally returning commonplaces singing value
Being the nookie of time itself whose destruction's gotta be total
The way time's production fakes my sustained distraction me

\- lody equals the boredom and the dead
Time producing you can be my fundamental security singing the sound
Of yr name having fallen out of every proper meaning system
So it might be mine or anyone's

— ~~*generality being otherwise totally fatal.*~~

ALL ROOF NO HOUSE

Calling back my dead to sheds in
Stately yards the cut's still fresh
No one would think to resurrect

My theft downs dawn & cinders
Like his eyes comport my beams
In you my time will be yr labor

No sky opens living meshes shiver
Trees go dead the dead go dig
- ing down my body's conquered

High above yr head they hang no
Eyes compost his beams in mine
Remains still air inters whatever

- 's real evicts no place to posit
Still ash waste & consequence
Whose hollowed mouths my in

- sides sing it out to you as if
To vomit this I am

— *only I when you cut here.*

TALKING POINTS

My work is one of gluing things becoming false a profligate
Skin amassing voice interrogation channels gluing useful lips
To mouth sublime oblivions lurk in things value hides not being
One w/ our optics my latifundia as if the problem were retinal
I'm screaming out *out vile jelly!* the occupier's in my eye being
A property of luster lipping & deceased little lichee nuts this is
The work of food vacancies linking hands perceived externally

As hate touching mouths I can't remember things but his limbs
Ingrown for channel jamming bodies clog no frame as hot lust
Fans sheer weight the earth imagines loins patch nerves drills stones
Exchange for skin what pure emotion stalls at the place I pucker in
- to public feeling moderation conceals extremist cores my heart
Being one a puny mushroom nothing can refer to what's lurking
Inside diminishing fields of prospect I get lost becoming sound

After periods of gross decay fish turn belly up in schools killed
By abstractions nobody made like his fibula nobody made any no
- ise as if the future were hanging on sounds no one hears move
- ments internalizing grinding down uncertain work the body
It goes lewd & limps the world entrenched inside dark rumors
Illuminating roads excessively lit for safety lives in market share
My vision security measures like prefab bulletproof periscopic

Infantry officiating form fed cognition annals chronicles all sent
- ient space whose culverts streaming sewage glows w/ such
Immediacy into which I keep coming without making contact.

AFTER MALLARMÉ

Pure & impenetrable a glamour today may be
A whack the thing's dumb wing will shatter us o
- bdurate lakc forgotten haunting under frost

This glassy edifice being as many flights unflown
Like a sign a swan remembers being itself a
- mazing how the thing cedes with no hope

While faltering so fucked-up it's failed to sing
Of living when tedium a sterile winter shines
And its whole neck shakes a blank agony still

Thrown by space upon what bird would deny it
Not this ground a terror where one's feathers are
Frozen old icy ghost by its brilliance assigned

To place this thing lay paralyzed with hatred
- 's frigid idea my song assumes

— so useless a deport.

COMMUNION

On one of our walks across the city this one
In May to the Champs Elysées where we'd other
- wise never go except that it was gorgeous a Sun
- day and there was only one big store

where we knew we might find the sound
- track to the film we'd seen the night before whose songs
We wanted to hear again a walk being the best pretext
For spending the afternoon in one another's company

and this was the occasion for my friend to tell me
That she recently realized how she'd been reorganizing
Her life in such a way as to enable a rapid response
To an unforeseen occurrence be it simple event or grave
Disaster a kind of confession that provokes for me

a question of scale insofar as multiple
Possibilities rush to fill that blank say on the one hand a sudden
Opportunity to relocate far from the density of electromagnetic
Waves characteristic of Paris with its unregulated con
- centration favorable to corporate telecoms
Proven to sicken & damage the body

in response to which my friend had com
- mitted her activist energies and on the other hand a collision
With an asteroid like the recent flyby of DA14 or the one
That exploded over Russia evoking a planet
Spectacularly colliding with the Earth at the end

of *Melancholia* which recalls Benjamin's chill
- ing insight at the end of "The Work of Art in the Age of Tech
- nological Reproduction" when he remarks on the way humanity
In the era of the Third Reich had made its own destruction
An aesthetic pleasure an idea I say to my friend

that places Lars von Trier's film
On a par with Leni Riefenstahl's *Triumph of the Will.*

BARREN TENDER

A plover's eyes my bored refrain whose diamond spits go divvy
Up the cash advance pay up they say shoot from the hip
Or be hocked we all drink in it the same pink lips all *bird de*
La mer in debt we're bundled small bills arctic pigeons secur
- itized words wank the woods so thick a thieving seeks ID in

- terior life being race profile externalizing error like a starry
Spit you can invest in pigeon force plover or whatever bird
You can eat me too or sleep inside my stutter a thing so pure
My own plover being so untrue the flesh I mean it suffers
A haze so dazzling a skin a soldier like frozen land the earth

Gone cold under money in the black or the red it's just the self
Same bird no more than coin can't see the things I pulverize

— *and so I've slept in yr report.*

ENCROACHING ON DESERT FIELDS, A HOUSE WILL HAVE BEEN BY NOW DESTROYED BY CONTEMPLATION

Not knowing how to cure a body his being
Taboo and cursed and cursing nature being dead
Like their land it's of the deadest dirt
Becoming people under phosphorus spells
White shells my waste disproportionately equals
What we eat seeing how we're all meat

                    - eaters now yr people I eat
The way I name things thrown to sea all my
Friends have this memory of me plain verso
Of event horizons fucking them hard doing good
Business in my panties where everyone's eating
The goods my ass hungers for this

                              possibility of turning
Real loss to future profit he says I feel no desire
For material vengeance when a kiloton widget
Can fulfill all my needs at once in solitary songs
No words return this soft appearance.

THE INSENSATE REQUIREMENTS OF MASS MEAT

Dreaming of tar sands bad specie
Lubricates the common being bit
- uminous leaves a boreal forest
A soldier on my bathroom floor
Wrapped in bright new sheets his
Cock a beautiful stain a pillow's
Exclusivity's only private affairs

Deprived of all my special needs
Look how everyone's behaving
Like me no one's acting in speech
Itself having become a lubricant a
Silent partner in the national *moi*
With household events losing this
Potential to illuminate flesh is just

A story historical time being so o
- ntic a mole inside divinity whorls
Turning property into a public
Concern or is it the other way a
- round all my facts & meanings
Things being literal voids distort
My feeble attempt to delete

— *undesirable populations along these lines of air.*

THE CHILL OF ENCLOSURE LEAVES ONE UTTERLY EXPOSED
after Carl Dreyer

Being staked jawed facing flak the flame
Can't tell the good from what's exchange
- d for goods no one wants yr body but
The face remains another story withheld
Organs shrink to trade weighs every
- thing is always talking talking wasting
Periods of darkness these times dim
- inishing shrines frac resource boning
With no body even sky's been possessed
By CloudShield & Crossbow technologies
Of torment longing to see a little piece
Of her hair the skin it's stuck to my bills
My balls all dirty money seeks to engulf
The words for this becoming walls over
- whelming what their names forget in us.

OF THE THREE NEGATED LABORS

Only waterboarding remains to move my tongue
In pleasure you can't resolve things having seen
The days' events repeating what little we had

Said because to see what means means seeing
Nothing having identified the self with a sum
A picture whose interests keep killing what I keep

Wanting to become everything's rising here can't be
True can't even mouth yr own sensation of drowning
Being what I said the sun over the earth it comes

— *and goes without a trace.*

•

Until you whispered the secret in my ear
Yr measures so slight a displacement so
Immeasurable as stone.

•

Like yr body's inner edge I feel things everywhere pure circum
- schisms surround me but whatever happened in the car my
Social vacancy fills with random abductions stories extending

Lonely from the day's bleak tone rows a landscape or whatever de
- scending points in space can't see how we've been thrown
Out of the thing's now blank interior it's always a gamble trade

Being no event no self-evidence inside the dispersion affects
You boy how yr organs go on finding me here as one who might
Still feel a distance even when living in the other room strung

Out between whose cries and the inner heat yr body leaves rim
- ming images lips limits what these circumcisions sing around
Me no more optical effects now pure pictures eyeing this

— *heaven.*

THESES, ON THE REMEMBRANCE OF THINGS TO COME

— there being no language for current events —

28

migrating cranes, whose lines of flight misalign what will have been with what'll be no more, a blank in the present, a positive void, this streaming hole, my dreaming sink

29

all space already occupied, abandoned futures being neither forgotten nor remembered, the blank being here and nothing being equal, a holding cell for military age males, a public john where you can fuck anything, as all our relations come into money, a time-bound column of timeless figures, the games we play with our weapons when we only exist in our acts, this sadness without measure

30

under normal conditions, the birds would return to the same tree season after season, but they've begun to stray & lose themselves in identical scenes of catastrophe where disaster is often submerged below vague thresholds of perception, irrupting on occasion inside certain words *sky bone hair glass* which no longer stand for any real thing as the world alters its appearance in relation to a string of sounds, so that now it all begins to look like [——] the active non-existence of the world we didn't make

31

futures externalize in carbon credits, indefinite holdings extinguish the day, a pair of pliers isolate the miraculous nipple, cutting off the same with a scissor, so when the water recedes, most things will have similarly lost their form, an experiment whose truth has yet to be discovered, a mass of unaccomplished acts

32

I can draw a cartoon head around the other and still not recognize the place where I live because home bears no resemblance to the bodies feeding me, the ones who labor in the dark, the vaults and cells, repeating my flight, what we never hear in negated life

33

there's no future more appalling than the one resembling yr own, he said, the one contracting me to myself, I think, the one I bet my dollar on

34

whatever will have survived, a lexical haze, it all remains, the sound of waste, a square or cell, yr very body, the mind's filthy place, our lives bear nothing else in common

35

staring into radical meat, it's the only time we have, he whispers, pressing my face to his words before dashing into the solar hut with Miguel when minutes later his cries ring out, the flip side of despair, being a certain lack of coordination, my clumsiness in pleasure, so far from terminal groin

36

this site emerges out of void material, the obvious lack of a car, the petrified signs of dominant life, a concrete slab in Gaza, a metal sheet he calls a roof, tho there is no house, a place of interminable delay, an interval or arrest where history gets derealized and language never comes

37

read this and come be with me [. . .] so alone here [. . .] want the pay to be good [. . .] or good enough so we can live [. . .] please respond now

38

what kind of fantastic survival do you have in mind?, the tribunal inquired, but this is nowhere and can't be heard by the ones under interrogation, being already dead, the tongue's mystique, property & theft, buried like a wedge between grope & scream

39

my informer affords me acquaintance with maneuvers, voluptuous jousts without the viewers ever suspecting any covert presence, proceeding very gradually with sulfur-tipped torches, the whole idea of a global commons pillaging the minds of those who'd overturn it

40

lost birds have been shown to produce unoccupied spaces, whatever lends necessary flesh to undo this fatal blank, this walled-in proscenium, my home, being where the bloody thing occurs

41

stripped, not naked, peeling away the quality of things, speculative transit from being to money and back again primed, his body on the floor, mute opposable evidence, contesting everything I write

42

there's nothing more devastating than finding the birds all gone, these traces of desire to make the thing that's not, each current of circulation leaving behind the sediment of its destructive force, peace itself being the mystified value of military victory

43

there being no language for current events, like any consumer-friendly notion of difference, my specialized form of writing won't be necessary after this period of darkness

44

working inside a vast domain, certain blanks go unfilled *her papers unfiled* consummation of our common place, or the clamor of it all converging in the future's own forgotten past, where all our relations to metal and corn, to all the ones we might have been, manifest and mask this time we live not living

45

common assumptions shot to pieces, the way a hollow steel bit bores holes in his limb and when removed takes with it a round chunk of flesh as long as the drill itself, having penetrated bone, and still no evidence of injury

46

the last word having yet to be said, the task of making conscious these tendencies, hiding from random fire, throwing stones, looting figs, caught erect inside a hut, a cement square removed from the scene of its own uncanny replication along the border of hearth & dump, junkspace of what will have been no place, this theater of inconsequence

47

it's as if the dead don't really die, having died the way birds appear, not being of the natural world, having ceased to exist without ceasing, they're nearly identical, but not the same as the real ones they undo, this imperceptible dislocation round which our world will once have been undone

48

now overturn this pious nonsense, whatever it takes to make concrete [——] concrete, negating the common sense of common good, writing this while chipping away at lacquer and rust, a faint impression of wings

THE RHETORIC OF BLOOD

He hated hearing last things. It was breath, the
quantity of oxygen in the blood.
The rhetoric of the blood. It presents itself directly to the senses.

Norma Cole, *Coleman Hawkins, Ornette Coleman*

"The rhetoric of blood presents itself directly to the senses." I jotted it in a notebook while listening to Norma read one evening and, moved by what I thought I heard, the sentence made its impression on my page without comment, undated & unlocated, as if everything about it were self-evident, as obvious as blood.

Norma's lines challenge common sense by arousing the promise of direct communication *false immediacy* between language, body and sensation. Rhetoric, however, which Aristotle defines as "the faculty of observing in any given case the available means of persuasion," is anything but direct in its struggle for common sense even as it threatens to capture the very thing it names. This reminds me of how a writer's body *expressive vehicle of communication* can be said to capture the histories it holds—"which have deposited in you an infinity of traces without leaving an inventory" (that's Gramsci)—obscuring the forces that allow a body's voice to be heard, or silenced.

In his *Rhetoric,* Aristotle distinguishes between the "special places" [*topoi idioi*] and the "common places" [*topoi koinoi*] of all discourse. For Aristotle, poetic figures, turns of phrase, extravagant metaphors and singular remarks are "special places," particular utterances or idiolectic confections appropriate in some forms of social intercourse but inappropriate in others. By contrast, "common places" are those linguistic expressions that lend themselves to any situation, locutions upon which so-called common sense depends and without which social discourse would be at a loss for coherent orientation: basic oppositions, like more & less, push & pull, sooner & later; or directions, like left & right, and the political antagonisms these directions sometimes connote.

Unlike common places, "special places" might mark scenes of intense pleasure and suffering whose singular expression locates a limit of shared understanding, a horizon of public intelligibility, making legible the separations—often maintained by domination & control—that sustain the very order *hierarchy* of the common and the special. Such singular expressions *what the common excludes* may sound dissonant, like a score performed by Ornette Coleman; or offensive, like a passage out of Kathy Acker; or incomprehensible, like a poem by Gertrude Stein; or lurid, like a page by Sade, wrong, perverse. But for Aristotle, such phrases are absolutely proper *belonging to one* and inassimilable to the common *shared by all.* If, however, what we hold in common has been negated, and what we share is what we've failed to make, then this distinction begins to erode.

In his *Journaux Intimes*, Baudelaire suggests that it would be an aesthetic and a social achievement of the highest order to create a commonplace, a cliché: "The creation of a commonplace [*un poncif*], that's real genius," he writes, "I must create a commonplace." And I would add: Anything to prove the proper false, to return what appears to be singular & sublime to the banal & ordinary, the strange to the familiar. Or could it be the other way around as the prosaic is shown to be perverse, the inconspicuous conspicuous, the unremarkable remarkable?

And so, common & special *commodity & artwork* collide and converge as Baudelaire makes clear in *Perte Aureole* ("Lost Aureole") where a poet-angel watches approvingly as their halo falls into the mud—"now I can wander about incognito, doing perverse things like ordinary mortals"—just as lyric poetry loses the illusion of its auratic insulation from the marketplace. Maybe it was Baudelaire's singular achievement to have reinvented poetry as a vehicle to traverse the frontier dividing the common places from the special places, disguising the one as the other, smuggling false goods, sabotaging an otherwise hardened border, or making it irrelevant.

A contemporary version of Baudelaire's allegory of poetry's fall from grace would need simply to turn the mud into blood. But whose blood would that be? And what would it communicate beyond its rhetoric, that is, beyond the spill & the bath, the shed & the shot? What would it mean for blood to speak? What would it say before kin & line, true & blue, first & test, money & debt, property & race? Or maybe the beyond of blood, like the "thing itself," is just another figure for silence. And is silence common or special?

How can rhetoric present blood as a direct sensation without reproducing the orders and hierarchies that make sensation intelligible in the first place? Does music do that? Can poetry? The temptation might be that of Mallarmé's bouquet when the flowers themselves are forever lost to the word "flowers," a rhetoric of double negation. Or maybe it's more like trying to sense Rimbaud's "silken seas and arctic flowers (they do not exist)," which the poet longs to feel, with senses unhinged, in a world whose carnage has ruined both seas and flowers with a flag of bloody meat.

Je n'aurai jamais ma main, writes Rimbaud in *Mauvais Sang* ("Bad Blood"): "I will never have my own hand," i.e., my body, my labor, my writing. Blood is a rhetoric, and it's always bad. It intercepts one's relation to the body's capacity and its expression.

Reading Hortense Spillers, I'm reminded how the "vertical transfer of bloodline" is sutured to entitlements and property—"the prerogatives of 'cold cash,'" she writes—and insofar as these things were denied the slave, even kinship and motherhood are negated by the rhetoric of blood as it converges with the brutality of trade. "If a slave begat children, there was not a law south of the Ohio that could stop the eventual sale to any brute with the money" (that's W.E.B. DuBois, in his biography of John Brown).

As I go on obsessing about how my most intimate desires are haunted by the most abstract relations—be it to soldiers or prisoners, migrants or laborers—I can hear in Norma's lines the echo of another proposition that's been haunting me, a proposition I recall neither reading nor writing—"an absolute distance lives inside the most proximate closeness"—suggesting again how the most mediated & the most immediate converge, and I feel myself straining to grasp this idea as if it denoted what is closest to my body while only exposing the obscurity of my own perception.

When routine has me thinking thoughtlessly about my pleasures and my pains as if my desires were self-evident to me—the way the significance of blood might be said to be self-evident, its communication of itself spontaneous & clear—an infinite field unfolds between the idea of my person and the feeling of my body, an expanse at once spectacular & sentimental, indifferent & personal, reconciled & ruptured, mediated & direct, the way my reflection reproduces the fictitious immediacies of common sense.

Like the appearance of an autopsy report *seeing with one's own eyes!* the rhetoric of blood is saturated with all the social relations concealed by forensics, severing tongue & song, bone & word, organ & utterance. Perhaps forensics is the perverse condition that undergirds what psychoanalyst Marion Milner refers to as "the too great enthusiasm for clarity," or "the separateness of the seer and the seen" (that's Adam Phillips reading her).

Opposites often persist in and thru one another, like clarity & opacity, the way positive propositions—say, "the rhetoric of blood presents itself directly to the senses"—coincide with their own negations. Were I to move inside the space of such a proposition as if it were a building, a feeling of falling excites my bowels as false floors open on an endless series of regressing surfaces under the infinite strobe of yay & nay, provoking the collapse I associate with a certain movement of thought that philosophers might call "the dialectic" when they separate theory from the body. I like thinking how I first grasped this movement of thought as a feeling in my stomach, not an idea in my head, as logic opens a chute in my pelvic floor and I plummet, returning concrete sensation to an abstract turn of phrase.

And as my organs plunge unmoored in the cavernous space I call myself, I orient my senses back toward an ever-receding horizon of disaster—the rhetoric of blood made flesh—whose history is coeval with the present, while I simultaneously direct my senses forward toward history's undoing *revolution* something my mind can only fail to grasp while struggling to resist that failure.

A plume of smoke, visible at a distance
In which people burn
(Oppen)

The rhetoric of blood might present itself directly only to the degree that someone's body burns inside another's sensation. Like its own rhetorical instrument, my body is replete with these feelings, every gesture making meaning in excess of what common sense perceives.

We want to say

'Common sense'
And cannot. We stand on

That denial
Of death that paved the cities.
(Oppen)

Like "common sense," the rhetoric of blood is shot-thru with a violent struggle for meaning and it can only present itself to the senses by silently disavowing the blood to which it refers.

Maybe "the rhetoric of blood" refers not to the senses but rather to the volatile space between our fragile figures, "the membranous precincts between our multiple bodies [...] where much is sounding and is also unsounded" (that's Selah Saterstrom, *Essays in Divinatory Poetics*), and while "sounding" might augur the disruption of common sense, "unsounding" persists and it can be as violent as a chokehold, the rhetoric of blood authorizing a cop's brutality.

Perhaps the analogy ought to be with film. But were I to say "the *image* of blood presents itself directly to the senses," would I be any closer to naming this rhetoric? I'm still left trying to sense the rhetoric of blood as if I could touch the space between framed images, the space that Tziga Vertov calls "the interval," the common place that structures perception, a film's plastic support, the space between sensations being inseparable from sensation itself, at once condition and betrayal of "immediacy," so to feel an image can only be to feel the structure of this feeling, a phantom sensation resembling the body that bears my name, a name carried on the tongue that calls to me as if I were leaving a voicemail to myself.

Lost between sentence and sentience *at once block & blank, obstruction & promise* I'm suspended in a void of sensation that the rhetoric of blood indirectly anticipates—"the dazed state toward which words incline" (that's Georges Bataille)—and the absence of suspense is unbearable. In this space, rhetoric threatens to anaesthetize my capacity to sense anything at all as it performs its hygienic function, cleansing language of its visceral trace in the flesh. So while "the rhetoric of blood" might profess to speak *of* the body, it can only do so by forgetting the violence that makes the body something that can be spoken *about.*

Perhaps what I'm circling here resembles more "the *grammar* of blood" because grammar, I've often thought, refers to a set of arbitrary conventions that govern *control* the relations between subjects & objects, a coercive affair of monitored agreements stabilized by custom. But insofar as subjects & objects are also structural positions in a social grammar, places occupied by particular bodies, arbitrarily determined and historically naturalized, the grammar of blood can be said to present itself directly to the senses, but only to those whose body experiences this presentation as violence.

As my senses incline toward our common place—be it prison cell or futures market, "the excess of our unfulfillment" (that's Danny Hayward)—an image circulates of a body baking on hot asphalt, "Faceless down in a puddle / In a collage of puddles" (that's Tongo Eisen-Martin), where "blood" absorbs a ruddy pool that spreads beneath the weight of sanctioned death. The body hangs in a place whose structure is framed by police tape *cordon sanitaire* where the thing I sense is the silence of blood, echo in a gulf, this blank in perception replete with a violence I do not see, coz "blood" is in the way. This is my theater of displacement, arousing whatever sensation it takes to awaken me from the rhetoric of what I can not feel, my body's amnesia.

In the face of this surface without a face, in a dream of dreamless nite, or a fog of fogless flight, in a rage muted by force, or a panic made feckless by verse, and fearing my inability to feel anything at all, I substitute his heart on my heart for his cheek on the pitch, his lips on my skin for his fingers on tar, his cum on my belly for his blood in the sun, my fantasy of intimacy, this feeble effort to destroy a bloody rhetoric, to return a feeling to numbed abstraction, tuning my body *atoning* so that I might come closer to a negated touch called care.

PORNOTOPIAS

1.0 The Ideal Brothel

1.1 Steven Marcus coined the term "pornotopia" in *The Other Victorians* (1966) to refer to pornography's conceptual purity, a purity akin to utopia's critical failure to find its referent in an already existing reality.

1.2 Curiously turning to Max Weber's work on bureaucracy, Marcus considers pornography as an analytical construct, or "ideal-type," both in theory and in practice. "The more distinct and precise the construction of the ideal-type," Weber writes, "the greater its abstract or unrealistic nature."

1.3 "There are ideal types of brothels," Weber goes on, "which are technically expedient from the point of view of police ethics, as well as those where the exact opposite is the case." I want to think about pornography in opposition to the police *morality* and a challenge to every "ideal type," not out of disbelief in what representation can idealize when it negates its referent, but rather because there is nothing utopian about the ideal-type of brothel, which, like the ideal-type of bureaucracy, has become perfectly consonant with concrete social life.

1.4 Put another way: What happens when the difference between "technical expediency" and its opposite breaks down and the ideal brothel coincides all-too-perfectly with state, police, & market, that old troika whose logic determines what can and can't be seen *our democracy of total visibility* calculated from within regimes of representation that force into the light of image, language, and law precisely what resists the violence of these things?

1.5 By the 1850s, Baudelaire had already discovered Weber's ideal brothel *avant la lettre* in the language of democracy—*liberté, egalité, fraternité*—which believed itself to be a socio-political reality. Baudelaire is prescient about this in his prose poem "Solitude," where he writes of social circulation with characteristically corrosive irony as "a prostitution I could call *fraternitary*, were I to resign myself to speaking the beautiful language of my century." Baudelaire knows that the promise of economic happiness is underwritten by ideological alibis for the exploitation of bodies and things. The working prostitute, for Baudelaire, is the only one who is honest about this.

1.6 "The literary genre that pornographic fantasies tend most to resemble," Marcus writes, "is the utopian fantasy. For our present purposes, I call this fantasy pornotopia." But pornography needn't *resemble* any genre, for it is one: and as a genre *institution & apparatus* pornography often binds the body to a future that condemns it to the reproduction of its past.

1.7 If pornography is structured like a genre of fantasy, maybe it resembles "the fantastic" as Todorov has written of it, a genre which hangs on the reader's inability to decide between the occult and the uncanny. In other words: Is all this really happening, or is it just the effluvia of my dreams *my nightmares* as they coincide with the shadows of noon?

1.8 There are too many fantastic utopian failures to think about, from Sade's *120 Days of Sodom* to Dodie Bellamy's *Cunt-Ups*. One of the virtues of these works is that they transport us beyond the trappings of "failure" in a world where the ideal brothel has already been socialized under the sign of "success."

1.9 It's only when porn takes genre as its rule-bound condition of possibility *and* a material limit to transgress that it can begin to work critically against a regime of representation wherein my most intimate relations *to my body and the bodies of others* are mediated by the most impersonal images, ideals, concepts, words.

1.10 Etymologically, a pornotopia is just a place where prostitutes work, so it's literally a site where people labor, and could reasonably connote any location where an exchange of bodies—money & value—is transacted, say, a factory or an office.

1.11 Pornotopia and pornography: Both participate in Jacques Rancière's "distribution of the perceptible" by parsing, segregating, limiting, disrupting, withdrawing, challenging, prohibiting, spectacularizing, and determining what is and what is not available to perception. By the same token, they can also agitate the senses, instigating perception beyond what has been encoded.

1.12 Conventional pornography reproduces a set of generic codes whereby it can police what can be seen and what cannot.

1.13 Following Walter Kendrick's resumé of pornography's history in *The Secret Museum: Pornography and Modern Culture*, porn becomes a "social problem" in the 19th century, a problem that can be linked to two events: 1) the excavation of artifacts from Pompei in an age of Victorian morality; and 2) the spread of literacy with the intensification of urbanization. The problem concerns where to locate the images, statuettes, and frescoes that depict explicit acts of sexual love.

1.14 As I imagine it, pornotopia not only refers to the illegal brothel where illicit sexual transactions actually take place, "technically expedient from the point of view of police ethics," but equally to the sanctioned place *here* where exploited bodies and relations can be seen on display, while others are occulted and absence itself is spectacularized.

1.15 Exhibit A (an illustration of what will never be illustrated here): The bodies of dead soldiers whose images have been withdrawn together with the language *autopsy report* that denotes those bodies.

1.16 Pornotopia might connote a sanctioned place where unsuspecting bodies are penetrated by ballistics as a matter of course, exchanged *sacrificed* in the name of self-preservation *perverted love* and whose pictures must not be seen nor accurately described.

1.17 Under conditions of US global militarism, everywhere has become this sanctioned place and shares features of "the secret museum" *aesthetics of the public secret* where forbidden knowledge *bodies & acts* is at once produced and occluded, and where contact with its effects *word & image* is at once offered and withheld.

1.18 Every representation assumes an itinerary independent of a final referent, and while this promiscuity *connotation* may be inconvenient for power's delusion of mastery, a one-to-one correspondence between word and world is the real threat to social well-being.

1.19 Pornography is always entangled in regimes of power & knowledge that seek to control a world of reference. But it is precisely as contraband that porn has a social and juridical function, reproducing or challenging the line between the perceptible and the imperceptible.

1.20 Foucault theorizes the double bind of excitability and prohibition aroused by the endless production of language about sex, and it's hard for me to forget the feeling of the Vintage paperback of *The History of Sexuality* in my back pocket during ACT-UP protests in San Francisco circa 1989. And while I don't know if I ever really had the book with me like this, I nevertheless remember clinging to it the way one might cling in desperation to a life buoy as it helped to save my otherwise sinking effort to grasp the dynamics of the pornographic regime we were up against.

2.0 Porn's Post

2.1 Porn might refer to any of the following: 1) a genre whose conventions reinforce public taste, even when it transgresses it; 2) "the becoming-language of sex and cum" (Angela Carter); 3) the semiotic contamination of the social body by way of illicit representations; 4) a symptom whereby perversities are created, measured, analyzed, controlled, and amplified; 5) an aesthetic limit whereby forms of art are measured for social acceptability, i.e. porn as the limit of art; 6) a market for commodities; 7) a political technology for identifying and containing pleasures & affects; and 8) a masculinist social apparatus for regulating the relations between space and vision (what can be seen and where), pleasure and surveillance, publicity and privacy (Beatriz Preciado).

2.2 All these possibilities suggest hardened norms and the conservative measures for reproducing those norms. This also points to one of porn's policing functions: to reinforce the privatization of bodies and pleasures. In other words, rather than profaning standards of taste, porn produces and endorses them.

2.3 Profit-driven porn is an apparatus for regulating the bodies & pleasures whose representations it disseminates. It aids & abets contemporary regimes of accumulation & dispossession by reinforcing the private subject of private property, consumer of bodies & pleasures alike.

2.4 At the same time, porn can assist the effort to defrock this proper subject, to deform the center of acquisition and control, to negate "the illusion of sovereign pleasure" (Beauvoir).

2.5 In other words, a radical post-porn challenges the logic of private pleasure, refutes the value of interiorized gratification, and displaces the motivation of orgasm as an end.

2.6 The Marquis de Sade first challenges this end as his writing champions the exteriorization of pleasure in social space *writing* which becomes the space of pleasure's ongoing narration, something orgasm can only interrupt. "Sade knows that orgasm is but a tribute paid to the norm of the species and is thus a counterfeit of the ecstasy of thought" (Klossowski).

2.7 For Sade, language itself becomes a utopia where the limits of the visible & invisible, the licit & illicit, undergo perpetual destabilization, the scene of a never-ending ek-stasis of being. This is the ecstasy of thought, and it might manifest as an obsession with narratives and stories that reconfigure the limits of relating.

2.8 Sade is already post-porn. The world represented in his novels exists only in just proportion with its language. Like Dodie Bellamy's *Cunt-Ups* more recently, Sade's transgression is the revelation of its poetry: "languages made of phantasms of themselves" (Bellamy). Sade's provocation: To make language useful in the only way it can become so, by severing it from the uselessness of reproduction.

2.9 Consumer pornography conserves and exploits the presumed essence of a certain aim-driven sexuality, which participates in the consolidation of a normally sexualized citizen. But what about porn that fucks with that essence, porn that lends a form to the unfulfilled place of the always inessential?

2.10 Rather than reaffirming an end-directed sexuality determined by dominant paradigms of sex and gender, post-pornographic writing—writing that deforms its ostensible referents while destabilizing the border between visible & invisible—can undo those paradigms by sensing *being affected by* whatever particularity *unnamed, unrecognized* that has been excluded in order to further consolidate that citizen.

2.11 In *Music for Porn*, this excluded particularity is the tagged body of a dead US soldier withdrawn from view, maybe in Afghanistan, maybe in Iraq. What would it mean to materialize *here* the unrealized place of that body *otherwise disposable* and my intimate relationship to it *otherwise unfelt.*

2.12 The semantics of "tag" are rich—touch, mark, ID, label, price, slogan—and the tag's corresponding social functions are just as prolific: not only the homophobe's slur, cop's inscription, and profiler's strategy, but also the graffiti artist's tactic, merchant's device, taxonomist's rule, networker's app, and children's game. And then there's the toe-tag to which the whole body might be eventually reduced.

2.13 My body is not my own. A militarized common sense has penetrated it, a language of money and arms whose usefulness converges perfectly with the uselessness of every commodity, and whose accumulation turns to precarity, ruin and waste. To decolonize this body can only mean to pervert it, that is, to turn it away from every propriety.

2.14 What might it mean to make a lyric poem the scene of that perversion, a sodomitical act *utterly useless* to recover the body from that reduction, and to make pornotopia this useless place committed to the reinvention of use.

3.0 Kathy Acker & Personal Life

3.1 It may have been with Kathy Acker that I first began thinking about porn in relation to my desire to write. One passage in particular from Acker's early novel *The Secret Life of the Black Tarantula by the Black Tarantula* remains salient, even as I've been living with it for a long time. In a chapter called "The Story of My Life," Acker assumes the persona of the Marquis de Sade and pilfers, appropriates, collages Sade's writings, together with passages from W. Lenning's biographical *Portrait of Sade*, and in doing so she scores a meditation on the contradictions and impasses around what she calls "personal life."

3.2 "I'm trying to get away from self-expression but not from personal life," Acker writes, "I hate creativity. I'm simply exploring other ways of dealing with events than ways my lousy habits—mainly installed by my parents and institutions—have forced me to act. At this point I'm over-sensitive and have a hard time talking to anyone. I can fuck more easily."

3.3 What the narrator here calls "self-expression" is one of those lousy habits, a fiction sanctioned by the institutions *structures of power* she's resisting. Acker's writing struggles against a gamut of such institutions—gender, family, money, law—together with the division of labor, and the whole economic system whose interests these institutions protect.

3.4 "Self-expression" implies a kind of spontaneity that often fails to recognize the way expression is constructed and mediated by the institutions Acker's narrator most abhors. Writing from within these structures, Acker sees identity as yet another institution whose violent strategies themselves masquerade as "self-expression." Acker's writing aims to undo that violence. Hence, *In Memoriam to Identity.*

3.5 For Acker, identity and self-expression obscure something else, something more "real," something she refers to as "personal life," which may have less to do oneself and more to do with that mediating body of impersonal forces *power & authority* that condition individual lives and constrain our collective possibilities. In other words, personal life is social life.

3.6 Acker's language refuses to countenance the common sense assumptions that occlude the real conditions of these lives and possibilities. Hers is a language of negation, a language "which describes yet refuses to be a language that is socially given" (referring here to Goya's visual "language" in her essay "Realism for the Cause of Future Revolution").

3.7 For Acker, "realism" is a language that wants to get at "the connections between the 'real' events, and the holes, the silences… the interstices through which all of us fall." Moreover, it's a language that wants paradoxically to articulate "places where language cannot yet be," like "chaos, or the body, or death" ("The Killers").

3.8 Acker's work is not only the record of a discrete person. It also registers the scandal of all our social pathologies, the determination of our tiny, fragile egos to keep otherness out by walling ourselves in, reproducing social divisions by immuring ourselves in the name of a social good called "security": the social good as social violence.

3.9 Acker's realism embodies the crisis of security. Her work shows how the material boundaries upon which security depends are always the effects of stories, myths, fictions. Rather than disavowing these stories, Acker embraces and displays their mutability, as well as their ability to register the contradictions that make them what they are.

3.10 Acker's insights help me to think about porn as any regime of representation where one's most intimate relations—be it to one's own body, or to the bodies of others—are mediated by the most impersonal images and discourses.

3.11 To begin sensing the social composition of a personal self requires that one reckon into one's perception—or into the very organ of sensation doing the perceiving (say, an artwork or a lyric poem)—the most impersonal forces, all of which simultaneously become and destroy whatever it is we might think of as spontaneous expression.

3.12 Upon first reading Acker, her work offered me an illustration of the violence of identity: the forging of a self thru endless processes of subjection, the rendering (rending & renting) of one's body as a fit subject, a violence submerged in any self-expression that disavows the social relations that force the self to express.

4.0 Music for Porn

4.1 It was at a reading that I gave some years ago when I first referred in jest to what was then a work in progress as my "music for porn." I said it so self-disparagingly: I can't write the actual porn, I mused as if confessing a weakness, I can only write its pathetic accompaniment, I can only supply its décor. At best, I said, my poems might become the equivalent of the mauve shag that graces the interiors of my favorite seventies fag films.

4.2 At the same time, with "music for porn"—as it soon transformed itself from joke to title—I wanted to imagine my poems having it both ways: accompanying porn *accoutrement or prop* and exchanging themselves for it (the way one might read the syntax of Mahmoud Darwish's *Memory for Forgetfulness*, at least as that title has been translates into English).

4.3 I was also thinking about music *for* porn in the sense of poetry being in support of it, while thinking of the pornograph's potential to do critical work beyond its profit-driven manifestations and imagining how I might contribute to that work.

4.4 "For" porn, too, in the sense of helping it, transforming it, returning to porn its power to desecrate, a power it has lost by becoming inseparable from the totally normative.

4.5 In other words, music for a future pornotopia whose rhythms and measures are not regulated by the violence of social reproduction, and whose affects are not wired to the militarization of everyday life.

5.0 Oppen's Things

5.1 At the other end of my thinking there's the relentless and haunting specter of George Oppen: "There are things / We live among 'and to see them / Is to know ourselves.'"

5.2 But what happens when the things that Oppen says we must see in order to know ourselves are bodies, bodies reduced to the status of things, often dead bodies, bodies withdrawn from view, bodies that can't be seen, the circulation of whose images has even been proscribed and rendered taboo as a matter of public policy?

5.3 In order to know a self in the place my body occupies, I need to see these things I cannot see, expendable bodies, corpses reified & withdrawn, the amputated limbs & prostheses of a social organism that is nonetheless of me, in me, for me: a social body whose organs of sensation have been severed, seemingly beyond repair.

5.4 "It is by such wholesale slaughters that the body politic shows only too clearly that it considers men as a mere collection of things" (Beauvoir).

5.5 "To see" might mean nothing more than to restore these things *bodies* to subjective relation *lyric's vocation* against the hemorrhaging of relation, against the mirroring of dead and undead forms, whose reflections *vampiric gaze in the mirror* otherwise fail to relate them.

5.6 To write lyric under such conditions and constraints is to create *fabricate* organs of sensation so that these bodies might be perceived and located in otherwise impossible *prohibited* relation to my own.

6.0 The Patient Body as Assemblage

6.1 How might a poem register intimacies for which there exists no proper subject, no proper discourse? Stein offers a model with *Tender Buttons,* and Dodie Bellamy follows up ninety years later with *Cunt-Ups.*

6.2 Concerning intimacies where the intensity of relation goes unacknowledged, unnamed & disavowed: How might a poem arouse such intimacies whose organization *off the page* would impede the penetration of bodies in geopolitical space?

6.3 This concerns the way my own well-being—the health & integrity, pleasure & satisfaction of my body—is bound up with others' losses in an incommensurate vulnerability, an unevenly distributed exposure to social violence that is impossible to share: all my disavowed and obscene intimacies.

6.4 Put another way, what might a poem sound like were it to perceive *arouse* a rupture in the continuity of suppressed relation—*history*—that makes these intimacies imperceptible?

6.5 "'My cock hardens in a soldier's wound,' a figural horizon, a ludicrous conceit *obsessive ridiculous perverse* which shapes a gesture, limns an imaginary site *would that it were only perceptible* where all the affects and feelings aroused in penetration congregate, awaiting transfiguration" (*Music for Porn*). These lines continue to haunt me as my poems organize themselves around a hole in militarized common sense, at once a placeholder for relations that can't be lived under current conditions and a nonsite obstructing my desire for those very relations.

6.6 "Into our most intense union the opposite feeling enters—disorder, the strangeness of what's happening to me. Tears don't stop but convulsions do. The more I need you, the deeper the estrangement, the stronger my desire—a defect in the movement of love" (Robert Glück).

6.7 How am I to feel the fate of my body as intimately linked to the fate of other bodies, bodies lost in scenes of conflict *inassimilable "facts on the ground"* be it a dead girl in Gaza, or a ravaged US soldier in Iraq, or a detainee at Guantánamo Bay, when images of their corpses, together with whatever language may exist to denote these bodies, remain withdrawn from circulation? How naïve is it to think that a poem might sabotage these frames while making our unavowable relations available to feeling and thought?

6.8 In my effort to run with some of these questions, I've nourished a notion I call *patiency*, which has less to do with the body as the sovereign scene of its own actions, and more to do with the body as a situation of suspended agency and disabused mastery. If this illusion of mastery is a privileged delusion, then patiency is its refusal.

6.9 For example: "A girl stops walking and lies down on a street in the opening scene of a riot" (Bhanu Kapil).

6.10 Patiency is agency's inverse and complement, and its mood is one of openness: open to touch, which is as much an openness to penetration as it is to the promise of care.

6.11 Longing for release from all predication *desire to become a body untagged* the patient refuses its identification as something terribly not its own. This is the body susceptible to uncoded sensation or unanticipated touch.

6.12 This idea of patiency finds an echo in Roland Barthes' idea of "the neutral": the paradox of an always already violent disruption of violence, the unmarketable suspension of conflict.

6.13 Being the *abject* of grammar, the patient defies the conventions governing the relations between subjects and objects (De'Ath). Exceeding the sentence—"with content more volatile than what contains it"—the patient is beyond being sentenced (Kapil).

6.14 The degree to which the patient body is exposed to harm may be the degree to which it is also receptive to forms of affection & care that refuse the market-bound laws of family & merchandise, laws that otherwise subject the body to violence.

6.15 The patient body is not a self-enclosed and self-evident fact, but a social process—in excess of skin & skeleton, fingerprint &

DNA, spasm & orgasm—and part of larger assemblages linked to other bodies locally and trans-locally, sometimes in zones that might seem very far away.

6.16 Patiency challenges the body's borders, the fantasy of which converges with a policing function. This means reimagining the body as a process without a center, not a discrete biological or social fact, but an untotalizable set of relations, the body not as a static object, but as the ek-static convergence of processes always in excess of themselves.

6.17 In "How to Talk About the Body?," Bruno Latour writes about the body as "a dynamic trajectory by which we learn to register and become sensitive to what the world is made of." But what is the world made of? While Latour remains symptomatically quiet on this question, one can answer simply and without fear of reduction: The world is made of laboring bodies, the mystified relations between them, and the geopolitical assemblages—*money, goods, war*—within which we're all lodged.

6.18 With this last admittedly simple proposition, it's possible to suggest a categorical imperative, not only for the body, but for the poem: Sense what the world is made of! In other words, conceive of the poem as if it were a sensory organ—*a patient body*—in the process of becoming affected *moved* by those bodies & assemblages, these holes in common sense.

7.0 Sensory Organs In the Process of Becoming Their Own Theoreticians

7.1 Often I return to a proposition from Marx's early economic and philosophical manuscripts where he discusses what it might mean to move beyond a social system of private property that alienates the body from itself. For Marx, the work of the human senses is historical, constitutive of both alienation and its overcoming.

7.2 The sensory organs are charged with the work of becoming aware—in advance of the brain—of the body's specific predicament inside that system of social relations called capitalism.

7.3 Marx writes: "The sensory organs have therefore become theoreticians directly in their practice." Because of their direct contact with the machinery of the world's making, the sensory organs are in a privileged position to access, register, and theorize *in their very functioning* the economic system ahead of our intellectual cognition, making abstract relations perceptible thru concrete sensation.

7.4 No doubt the young Marx understood that only the body can yield the raw sensation for any future beyond the present's predations, and this proposition harbors a whole theory of aesthetics in relation to political economy.

7.5 What if we were to think of the poem as a kind of sensory organ? What might it mean for a poem *prosthetic organ extending from the body* to theorize *in its very practice* its predicament in a field *street* of sometimes imperceptible relations?

7.6 To be an *articulate* body—a body capable of relating to other bodies—means to be moved by other bodies and to perceive the relations that position our bodies in social space. But when these relations become so abstract as to appear supersensible, the body risks becoming inarticulate, incapable to relating, connecting.

7.7 The more connections and links *articulations & mediations* we are able to make, the better our perception becomes. This is a way of thinking about the cognitive capacity of the body.

7.8 Pornotopias multiply the body's articulations while registering its connections with other bodies. This implies being affected by otherwise imperceptible differences in an effort to perceive, always, as if for the first time, what a body can do.

8.0 What can a body do?

8.1 I want to take seriously the well-worn maxim from Spinoza's *Ethics*. "The body," Spinoza writes, "solely from the laws of its own nature, can do many things at which its mind simply boggles!" (*Ethics,* III, Prop. 2). Spinoza's proposition is frequently cited—"we still don't know what a body can do"—a symptom of our utopian desire for another world whose point of departure is a potential we already embody, here, now.

8.2 But Spinoza's proposition can only be rehearsed as a useless diversion *an apology* if it's not guided by the realization that we *do* know what has been done *to* bodies—from gender to genocide—and the mind can only boggle at what is being done to them now.

8.3 In an effort to perceive what a body can do, we might want to conceive a multiplication of its links in a perverse articulation of bodies that would allow otherwise inaudible social material—intimate relations whose intimacies go unnoticed, say, between my body and the body of a woman in Indonesia who made my shirt, and the body of a boy killed by a drone in Afghanistan, and the body of a migrant worker who harvests my tomatoes, and the body of a soldier disrupting a family in Iraq—to become audible as something other than a scream.

8.4 How can I imagine "the body"—after Civil Rights & Feminism, after Gay Liberation & ACT-UP—not as a transparent datum of knowledge, but as a critical obstruction inside these obscene networks of property and control, something opaque and resistant to identification *policing* a form of life in the process of mutation *unsanitized, unhygienic* a lifeform paradoxically committed to undoing its own conditions of possibility.

8.5 How to arouse *organize* this body in one's work not as the site of identity's recrudescence and expression but as the nonsite of ongoing displacement and mediation? The body not as primal property *my body* but as an incoherent set of relations always in the process of becoming its own theoretician. This is the body as a situation *already collective* where so many social processes, institutions & apparatuses collide: medical, military, economic, ecological, linguistic.

8.6 Inside these institutions & apparatuses *guarantors of my being* what does it mean to risk everything we think we know we are?

9.0 The Pornograph as Form

9.1 Pornography inscribes and polices the divide between the licit & the illicit, the visible & the invisible, the possible & the impossible, but it might also undo these oppositions.

9.2 As a complement to the potential of the human senses to feel their own historical predicament, the pornograph has the potential to register the body's socio-political situation by articulating *linking* it in seemingly perverse configurations and strained syntaxes that challenge commonplace divisions: normal/pathological, public/private, militant/military, impersonal/intimate. That is, the pornograph has the potential to intervene in the way all these categories are constantly being produced, distributed and reinforced as common sense.

9.3 Put still another way, the pornograph might risk concretizing the body's abstract relations to other bodies, phenomena, and processes. These are patient bodies, open to perceiving how they affect other bodies, and vulnerable to being affected by them.

9.4 Consumer pornography is the most conservative of image systems—"ruled, regulated, produced and abused by pro-capitalist assholes and white straight men selling their boring desires through ideas of liberalism and democracy" (Tim Stüttgen)—and what it conserves, even at its most perverse, is the discourse of normative sexuality, violent guarantor of social reproduction.

9.5 The social potential of the pornograph: To stimulate an irruption into that discourse by perceiving something in excess of its regime, something unthinkable within its terms.

9.6 At the same time, the excesses of the pornograph might potentiate the perception of social relations otherwise so withdrawn in scenes of occulted labor and hidden detention—factories, fields, and prisons—and whose seeming distance from the visible carries an intimate proximity, call it the social obscene. Arguably, these relations require the extremes of generic representation to condition the possibility of sensing something beyond the reach of genre. The pornograph might then become a placeholder for all my unseen intimacies.

9.7 This is the radical fantasy of the pornograph: To render the private self as improper, lewd & offensive.

9.8 Pornotopia, then, not as a critique of the mediated quality of our social relations, but rather the place where the body can appear saturated with all its occulted mediations.

9.9 Considered in this way, pornotopia would be opposed to the ideological delusion of immediate perception (common sense). The more mediations with which we saturate the social space of appearance, the greater the possibility for rendering the impenetrable intelligible.

9.10 "The recognition of impenetrability houses the hope of intelligibility" (Oppen).

9.11 Pornotopia: The placeless place where the body can contest the terms of its articulation, the body as means without an end.

9.12 The promise of porn to defile is a promise betrayed by its conservative bent to eroticize the paradigms and apparatuses that already identify & subject, capture & police us.

9.13 Disabling self-enclosed delusions of sovereignty, porn might still recover its promise to undermine the very divisions it erects, potentiating new bodies & pleasures that fuck-up the meanings of old sanctities. This is the promise to profane aim-driven sex, which the whole apparatus sanctifies in its most amplified terms: the money shot as evidence of desire's fulfillment, distillation of capital's dream about itself.

9.14 At once infinitely removed from and intimately entwined with the body of a dead Afghani mother killed by a drone, the body of a dead US soldier killed by an IED is perhaps the most inassimilable body, the body most indigestible by the US media spectacle. But these bodies have been paradoxically absorbed by the very apparatus that excludes them while spectacularizing their absence.

9.15 Like a tremor of apocalypse *revelation of the body's canceled potential* the pornograph can alternately become a tactic for undermining those same hierarchies and machines, insinuating inassimilable bodies and pleasures into orders of invisibility and surveillance.

10.0 The Specificity of a Queer Pornotopic Subject

10.1 Porn arouses a utopian edge where narrative, commodity and community converge at their marketable extremes before exhausting themselves, hemorrhaging in an excess at once produced and recuperated by a market where the potential for non-monetized forms of social life has been caught inside monetization itself.

10.2 Market driven porn isn't categorically oppressive and hegemonic. At its best, queer porn can appropriate the apparatus of pornography to elaborate specifically differenced bodies, longings and subjectivities. One can use the machine to potentiate the breakdown of the very identities that the apparatus produces, to disable one's own subjection. This could be porn's social function, often offering the only reservoir of images that reflect one's desire in a society that has pathologized it.

10.3 At its limit, gay male porn becomes a perfected formalism where a typology of marketable masculinities is celebrated as a pure construct, empty of any essential content.

10.4 Porn exteriorizes character as de-psychologized persona and social artifice. Robert Glück talks about this in an essay called "Caricature," that is, the way porn sets up character systems and social typologies "in order to tear them down" as the body coded and conditioned by legible type collapses into its opposite: the body in orgasm shorn of stable social identity.

10.5 While parodying forms of social identity—many of which are anchored in labor *identity as work* from taxi driver to chauffer, secretary to businessman, plumber to architect—porn reinforces a logic of disintegration and the need to break up social reality if only in order to satisfy desire. The problem, of course, is that what gets broken is as easily repaired, if only to ensure that it can be broken again.

10.6 Mainstream porn is therefore inadequate to alter the relations that ensure the ongoingness of pleasure's bad infinity. Porn then becomes yet another negative imprint of utopia as it simultaneously arouses and constrains the promise of democratized pleasures.

10.7 In commercial porn, identity functions as currency & lubricant, so when its exchange function is consumed, or when the orgasm it produces is consummated, its usefulness is exhausted, if not destroyed. And here lies the beautiful contradiction of pornography's death-drive: Just as eros dissolves identity in sex, so too does commodity liquidate one's instinct toward self-preservation.

10.8 While porn often sheds light on the contradictions of identity and its undoing, it nevertheless remains complicit in reproducing the terms of a broken reality whose norm is precisely relational dissolution. Unable to transcend its own commodity status, porn nevertheless registers, senses and perceives, a faint desire toward the utopia it blocks.

10.9 Insofar as regimes of domination are normalized by cultural fantasies, I wonder if fantasy can be aroused to awaken our perception of otherwise imperceptible structures of domination and one's place inside them.

10.10 Even as it harnesses one's desire within an objective system of exchangeable bodies, most porn lacks a corresponding subjective element that might challenge that system, because to challenge that system might threaten to undermine one's access to pleasure.

10.11 One might begin to theorize porn's limit in the absence of what Ernst Bloch calls the "subjective factor," which he argues is crucial for any utopian form to make a countermove against society's "bad existence" as it normalizes and reproduces itself. The subjective factor is critical in any effort to arouse "those contradictions inherent in the bad existence in order to overcome that existence, in order to bring it to the point of collapse."

10.12 This is why porn often only impedes its own desire "… to transcend the contradictions implied by any demonic system" (Beauvoir).

10.13 I'm reminded here of something I learned from Earl Jackson regarding the revelatory bathhouse passage in Samuel Delany's *The Motion of Light in Water* (1988). The scene is set in 1963, in the pre-Stonewall St. Mark's Baths, and it narrates the writer's social and political awakening on the threshold of "that gym sized room" replete with an "undulating mass of naked male bodies spread wall-to-wall."

10.14 This is a moment of radical social discovery and self-formation, identity not as deep psychological image, but rather as the recognition of oneself as a politicized subject in what would soon become a social movement. As Delany notes, "It was a 50s model of homosexuality," that he was then on the verge of overcoming, a model "that controlled all that was done, by both ourselves and the law that persecuted us—homosexuality was a solitary perversion."

10.15 Upon seeing what was otherwise isolated and unspeakable, perceiving on a mass scale what had been relegated to the isolated and fragmented, Delany connects private sensation to public perception and politicizes his experience for the first time. No longer would he measure the self-evidence of sexual encounter against prevailing 1950s representation of homos as isolated perverts.

10.15 Bathhouse as pornotopia: Delany's scene is pregnant with a future of somatic plenitude and political power.

10.16 Delany narrates this moment as an awakening to oneself as a socially aware sexual subject, while refracting the telling thru the present tense of his narration in AIDS-riven 1988 when the social movement that he intuited in 1963 on the threshold of that gym had been pressed to serve the current ends of self-preservation whose demands were already hardening around newly codified norms and monetized identities.

10.17 Despite what might have seemed to be the abandoned future of the past's concrete utopia, Delany hews to that burgeoning scene as one of visionary promise. "If I may indulge in my one piece of science fiction for this memoir, it is my firm suspicion, my conviction, and my hope that once the AIDS crisis is brought under control, the West will see a sexual revolution to make a laughing stock of any social movement that until now has born the name. That revolution will come precisely because of the infiltration of clear and articulate language into the marginal area of human sexual exploration."

11.0 Sade's Value

11.1 Reading my "Obscene Intimacies" from *Music for Porn* aloud in pubic for the first time I feel like I'm gonna be sick, like I'm on an interminable ambulance ride from the site of geopolitical trauma to the morgue.

11.2 Two details from the early sections of *120 Days of Sodom* feel crucial here. The first is the emphasis Sade places on the ear as the most critical organ of sensation *theoretician* for it is the organ penetrated by language. The second is the emphasis placed on narration itself.

11.3 As modeled by Sade, pornotopia is a place of storytelling that activates *arouses & multiplies* as many points of mediation *points of narration* as possible. The more numerous and searching in its details, the more scenes of the body's articulated connections—points of contact between bodies and bodies, bodies and language, bodies and systems, bodies and institutions, bodies and power—the more enhanced our chances become to sense the unrepresentable whole.

11.4 The body is in excess of every ordering system *value & language* determined to harness and contain it, just as those same systems exceed the body.

11.5 This is the value of Sade: His writing disrupts every appeal to whatever imagined future is necessary to guarantee the present's value.

11.6 Whereas Sade is faithful to language, relentlessly drawing our attention to its endless proliferations, straining physiological and social syntax *the composition of bodies in space* I want to be faithful *impossible* to those bodies whose deaths *by IED & IDF, by strike & drone* create a seemingly unrelatable excess, bodies without a common sense to relate them to myself.

11.7 Sade offers a radical parody of enlightenment logic, a logic of universality that would find its full realization on the guillotine, where the value of liberty *money* can be affirmed only at the expense of every particular *dissent* which threatens to pervert it. At the moment of the "Declaration of the Rights of Man," Sade undoes the abstract value *false equality* of "the human."

11.8 Finally, Sade's writing contests the universality of human experience by registering the rejected particular *the patient of dissensus* that undermines the false universal of hygienic *militarized* reproduction.

12.0 This Organ Opens One to Structure

The situation's pretty unstable
Said my soldier with no hands
And I imagine his prosthetic

Up my ass I love the feeling I
Even quiver with the pleasure
Of being

— so near the goal.

Works Consulted or Referenced:

Kathy Acker "The Killers"; *The Childlike Life of the Black Tarantula*; and "Realism for the Cause of Future Revolution." Giorgio Agamben, *Profanations*. Roland Barthes, *The Neutral*; and *Sade/Fourier/Loyola*. Simone de Beauvoir, "Must We Burn Sade?" Dodie Bellamy, *Cunt-Ups*. Ernst Bloch, *The Utopian Function of Art and Literature*. Angela Carter, *The Sadeian Woman and the Ideology of Pornography*. Amy De'Ath, "L(a)ying Down in the Banlieue" (*Metamute*). Samuel R. Delany, *Motion of Light in Water: Sex and Science Fiction Writing in the East Village*. Robert Glück, "Caricature"; *Margery Kempe*. Earl Jackson, Jr., *Fantastic Living: the Speculative Autobiographies of Samuel R. Delany*. Bhanu Kapil, *Ban en Banlieue*. Walter Kendrick, *The Secret Museum: Pornography in Modern Culture*. Pierre Klossowski, *Sade My Neighbor*. Bruno Latour, "How to Talk About the Body?" Steven Marcus, *The Other Victorians: A Study of Sexuality and Pornography in Mid-Nineteenth-Century England*. Karl Marx, *Early Economic and Philosophic Manuscripts*. George Oppen, "Of Being Numerous." Beatriz Preciado, "The Architecture of Porn: Museum Walls, Urban Detritus and Stag Rooms for Porn-Prosthetic Eyes," in *Post/Porn/Politics*. Jacques Rancière, *Dissensus: On Politics and Aesthetics*. Gerald Raunig, *Art and Revolution: Transversal Activism in the Long Twentieth Century*. The Marquis de Sade, *The 120 Days of Sodom*. Tzvetan Todorov, *The Fantastic: A Structural Approach to A Literary Genre*. Tim Stüttgen, ed. *Post/Porn/Politics: Queer Feminist Perspective on the Politics of Porn Performances and Sex Work as Cultural Production*. Max Weber, "'Objectivity' in Social Science."

WEAK LINK

— the 'spontaneous' element represents nothing more than an incipient form, analogous to the arousal expressed by all the old poems and distractions; but before dealing with the literary manifestation of this overvalued element, it would be wise to note the following characteristic possibilities, which throw some light on our conflicting tendencies —

LEGEND

[——] ≠ place of future action, being choked inside a tube, only the weakest

[——] ≠ surviving scenes of this undoing, a blank, or common place, bodies wash up

[——] ≠ inside my interior, being a question of waste, remains, and all that can't

[——] ≠ survive environment, now subtracting a false irruption of birds, the buzz

[——] ≠ a null expanse, a local undoing, undermining refuse, enhancing relations

[——] ≠ no remnant, equaling waste, disseminating methods, eventuating seed

[——] ≠ futures, markets recall the body to itself, having been this thing surviving

[——] ≠ identity's dreamy excess, in thrall to message, achieving no place

[——] ≠ a hut, a border, a line, a tree, a method, a dead boy in Gaza, or any residual

[——] ≠ subject, an unstoppable irruption, a tailbone poking thru environment

[——] ≠ this skin, undoing what the war forces

— *weakening the links.*

Being so vehicular, roomy where my feet are
Tanks arrive inside, this way of picturing
Tall things go on lurching, limbs macerate
In public we reckon impossible tense, shame

On our own white floors, becoming impossible
Bodies extracted by the thousands, amassing
In a vault, margins, or a full-time occupation
These precedents bulk, my binding theme

•

Occurs, there being no such place as this at all
The imputation having been determined
So many erroneous self-images [——] skins
The hair and nails, our missing mortars, stumps

Here we feel pressing [——] the loss of woodland
Scenery sinking under national, yr transmission

•

Just bellies up and dies, goading future publics
Modular blocks [——] becoming girders, buildings
Frozen speech, unrecognized as the material
Beneath which all the stone, the wall, the white

Spreading over something, under the influence of
[——] can we say 'the sum of human resources'
A gutted corpse uncounted, being one among
These things careening into tall & standing others

Now let's fall-out into truth, go lob anything that throws
The desiderata of remembering the present for some
Example of being I'm sampling my latex hose for pores
Evidentiary leaks, where it all appears likeminded

To withstand so virulent a strain, all knives and spoons
We staple to our chests like armor, what sickly streams
All bleached [——] a shrill though fatal thud suppressed
A patch of hair or anything to stand on, now standing in

•

For [——] or against, such breathtaking disproportion
[——] a sense of can't be gathered up in scales

And in all these faces, the stills turn dark side up
Crushed to sand, a pink opaque erasing every sign

•

Of local need, the question of place remains beyond
Recognition [——] there being no foundation for the thing
To come, flooding tens of thousands, respectable merchants
All doing capital business when the awful news dissolves

Exchange, alluvial folds, our degraded interiors
        [——] shaping mutual alleviation, strains of want

                Diminishing, what you hear is the erosion
                        [——] of sound, this decay of tone

•

Now stand by our withering stately
Ways increasing daily forces squander
Fuels my harnessed links impeded

Heavenly connections trading soft
Targets doing business in [——]
Absentia where my migrant sleeps

In clandestinity to earn a patch [——]
Of hair or something taped illegal
Missing parts becoming real

Live guest-workers pump it up
I'm all you'll ever need, he said
A bloodless thing my dildo stalks

— *the new faux nation.*

•

But it all gets even creepier still [——] stirring
Deep inside us there is perishing, or something
Looming under legal methods jet black wigs

Destined to what this destiny can't contain
It's really hardcore, the social being merely so
Many oppositions de-linking [——] wedged deep

In styrofoam, my needles and the jugs break down
Being tour of duty, an avenue of ingress [——] tracks
Separate from the land upon which we move

Big dollar contracts icing jelly flap profits
Over time, there's nothing lurking deep inside
Resource [——] keeps it all intact until the day

All this appears in what appears to be still
Separating [——] love, or anywhere to hang
Yr face turns real grub to fake adventure

[——] pumping my disturbance with phonation
Days go by, open vowels, not generating much future
Sound [——] losses where all this will have happened

Any common place [——] strung out on being still
Produced disfigured gently now my ratcheted dejecta
[——] his leg becomes my fluted stump, my lip

His anal spur [——] missing tongues insert the word
Whose shock force grids resistant salvage, ours
Being squandered in advance, we molt in network

Fibers, having traced the place of future action
What can't be named in a field of roots, so come
Inside my fjord of mannered stools [——] watch

•

— *the eyes peel back, so pasted to the blazing.*

So weak, these lines achieve that TV blue
Spanning whole vast global souths my geo
Graphic underbellies really want to
[——] fuck, stringing teeth to foreskin

Rituals, trade pursuant to whatever
You excrete [——] a fair exchange, or
Just say botox and I wet my pants

— this is about being craven in a carapace.

•

Come deeper now and kiss a little facial gum for steel
How yr system's beauty hovers in me, so shameful
Like rain clouds all the block-womb, antecedents
Boasting excess [——] this is fantastic, privation

In the language of plowmen, these extra folds
Skin and how we faked the needed hat disguise
Persona at the border, or some little article wedged
Between this failing organ [——] and that one

Opportunity shimmies slender faults to sanctum
I put my finger in his flap [——] still pulling back
For more, a so-called viscid white emulsion, or what
Ever it takes to make the ordnance take its target

Anything to ensure the proper bonding
Sickens in dehiscing blanks, a thickening
Trace achieves salvation [——] withering away
Gazing at events we still can't name

— *and these have named us.*

The system and its structures speak
Of dwelling and old utopian profiles
[——] penetrate us like architecture

Or something standing in erecting
All these needs for dwelling swarms
New feed dislodging shelter trades

The rent will not exhaust the ground
Vast huts my love's all gone to weed

— *the land, whose fateful portion.*

All but laminate remains to chafe
Insensate shares the grainy waves
Our phantasms stoke a pretty deal

These facts constitute what sanctions sanction our reports.

[——] = a common place we can't sense, but upon which all we
perceive depends

•

Now give me anything but a concrete role
[——] no longer generating the materials, ore
Whatever's necessary to make this moment
A null one, being real as walls displace horizons, mass

— compressing insides, so vaulty and voluminous.

•

Networks [——] fill my open trench
The filament & bulb, marked by a sliver

Something deeper still

[——] my silver

putsch.

•

Shrill accords record [——] all these vibrations
Miming better reproductive techniques I have
Sown dark clouds above our bed the beautiful

Sounds of circuits memory and capital my treat
- ment of the subject won't save us from the total
Oblivion in becoming objective social fact

Collecting all the names and occupations
Yr sex will have been one of these [——]
Exhausted periods of glaciation coming from inside

The blanks I mirror his missing sounds all lip & throat
Compensate deficiency diminishing waste
[——] now admit our activist elements

— *being nameless, we can sabotage the goods.*

Unaccustomed stills to all the muted
Interest in this global aphasia my
Amnesia's just not clinging like we used to
Be [——] recalling things so desperately

Standing in for others like erosion
Taking place without the place itself I
Being this sudden downturn in production

— *unable to avert the peril ourselves.*

— or just relate the thing upon
The table to the process of its making
Noting lines the minted substance

Imputing something even vaster
Clinging up inside the skull
Our speech disturbance still

— *in motion.*

•

In place of something stands here, I, being serial
Dissent, attachments falling into salt-flats pumping
Up the so-called 'actual interconnection of all things'

Being a little blue today, green's the color, my terror
Alert all soft electrics, query cables crush the hold
Pursuant to what moves in waves, I'm harder still

Our gunboats spell a little haze above my stanza lags
There being way more beauty in that amputee than any
Cash could lend this place some real appeal

For all the off-shore crude, drilling broken facial steel
Limits no one credits for the mysteries of our turf

•

But democracy won't occur before the curfew
Blackens my diminishing force, elemental
Skins glow, organs crave yr foresworn illegal
Touch, they've traced powder in our stools

Therein lies the nation's intelligence, a gap in stills
More fortified [——] lands remain to be cracked
Opened pillaged traversing starved ignoble nature
Remind me now which headscarves to avoid

What mongrel forms to put to sleep, exchanging
Yr sex for contracts at the county seat, waving
Facts, titles [——] these airs get funneled into deeds

— *without the promise of their stain.*

Out-posting there on a patch
Their missing parts become us
Being less than concrete roles
We're turning up remains [——]

The commons being waste my
Disposal capacity's running low
On ethanol fuel blends coming
From the south the outcast
Eats my shit

— *so to speak, etc.*

Recoding all this and the wonderment in that

Grafting enhanced tissues
New things to make the body prolix
Trading two appealing little coats, legs inside
Their insides [——] there being nothing more

— *to describe here.*

•

Now from the moss at lower elevations
[——] new monetary excitements come
Devouring the blanks exchanging signs
Trace nourishment, axing out our edifice

Lighten up yr load, recent avenues blocked
By the war or what stands in for [——] that
Being blocked by two bodies nobody saw
What's coming, being immaterial, he said

The crisis just reconstitutes what's known

— *events now battered into bone.*

Even if you don't like housework, he said, you may
Still court tendencies to overdo things sometimes
Like sucking cock in corporate coffee booths
Bunkers, unprotected factory floors, remains

No civic foundation, recombining activities to beat
The system with low wages, money saving coupons
We can really organize & shop for two, or more
If we could only share some of this wealth [——]

But he seemed sincere, and I wasn't thinking
Anymore about the war, or the local hunters
Who say they'd love to take us bone-fishing

— *anytime can really help you unwind.*

•

O what I'd give to penetrate some inner pooch
Such lining, furs excited girders
Darkened screens, my hut's a poking thru

bone-refined

the nation's sorry ass

out-posting to the

[——]

bitter.

•

I'm afraid [——] there's nothing more to say
From here we've been detained, as in a car park
And y're under [——] ground transmission
Spreading thru channels of our capillary

Mediations [——] there being nothing more
To apostrophize or summon, hails of nature
It seems so desperate, seeming still so hardened
No message lost in the overproduction of signal

Lost in my ear pressing up against yr hollow chest
Old nonsite of delinking breath & word the scene
Of soldiers' bodies looted senses might report

•

the peculiar odor of our [——]

odium.

rain today, just need a little something to funnel down
the spine, it's this peculiar odor of dust, and ocher rising
from the softer growth, where some relation begins
to cohere, a place where no one lives anymore

I was thinking all this under duress & up against the wall
wondering how we ever got from then to now

having merely said this, having said this

OF BODIES AND WASTE

Dearest Z. - I'd be lying were I to say I wasn't bewildered by yr insistence that I "analyze" my own poem for you, as if the thing weren't clear already. You had asked me to address what you believe to be its blatant obscurities, and while I was loathe to indulge yr query on the occasion when you made it—that table around which we sat under soporific office light felt way too judicial, like we were in a law court, hence my paralyzed withdrawal—I've since decided to give it the benefit of my doubt, and respond in earnest as if you'd asked it without hostility.

Line by line, the poem you're questioning seems kinda transparent, tho I can see how the shifting frames of association create a stony effect in their aggregate:

Wetlands and marshes slow.
But my poems, like *phynance*
— this accumulation of waste —

Okay, so the first line's a direct quotation from a report in the wake of Hurricane Katrina and refers directly—if but telegraphically—to the erosion of the wetlands along the Gulf Coast of Louisiana. Wetlands and marshes slow the breaking storms as they reach land, thereby offering some protection to the coast. As those wetlands erode, the local ecology becomes evermore vulnerable. The poem then conjoins and juxtaposes these wetlands and marshes with "my poems," articulating an unlikely relation between poetry (in this case my own) and the Louisiana wetlands, suggesting something of poetry's inability to protect us from disaster. This gets at something regarding poetry's social function, an idea that finds its elaboration in my naive simile, "like *phynance.*" The strange orthography of that word really did appear on my page out of nowhere & without explanation, but in it I could hear—as I've said elsewhere—the concatenation of physics, finance, and the natural ecology of phyla. By way of this one word—which could be a poem all by itself—my little lyric continues to sense and make audible the unnatural disaster of late financial capitalism, which dominant common sense takes to be part of nature's innocent design. Thru that intermediary term, phynance, the tercet concludes by relating "my poems" to both "accumulation," which names the illusory end of financialized production, and "waste," which accords with the latter's social & material effects: disposable populations. Maybe, now that you've gotten me thinking about it, I ought to have written, "this accumulation and waste," if only to suggest how accumulation *is* waste, I mean, the commodity itself when its value bears no resemblance to use, the way time accumulates in things together with labor, or the waste that's become of the human body reduced to carnage in wars, the body exiled to nowhere—the solitary hole in prisons—be it bandaged or banned, the body as offal or the body as money, meat or contraband, a Yemini detainee at Guantánamo Bay or a Black man in Cleveland whose bodies can be killed without being murdered.

I mean *this*, you and 'the cranes
Like ships,' they're relentless
— targeting flows, pipelines —

The whole set of relations that the poem sets in motion pivots on this "*this*"—*I mean what I'm saying! I mean this poem! I mean this poem is an accumulation of waste!*—and *this* is useless, and maybe the value of "my poems"—and poetry more generally—hangs on this uselessness. But, you might rightly add, so does the value of any commodity, which also contains the stuff of our negated commons: work, resource, relation. On the one hand, our living labor as writers of useless poems goes by the wayside, circulating without value outside productive channels of exchange, a kind of waste; and on the other, the work of poems remains caught up in the very structures of social economy and divisions of labor that aid and abet disaster itself. You know what I mean. Unlike wetlands and marshes, my poems do nothing to protect against crisis, and in their fragile disguise as "natural resource"—expression—they probably resemble phynance more than any abstract resistance to it. Maybe this is the kind of "radical mimesis" I'm interested in. But more to the point: Our logos—language & logic—participates in constructing and reproducing the very things that are killing us, and this is a truth I don't think poetry can afford to forget without indulging in the pride of deluded transcendence and narcissistic oblivion. And so the poem goes on, after the line alluding to Kalatazov's amazing film, *The Cranes are Flying* (USSR 1957), and its comparison between the natural world (cranes) and economic production (ships), to extend this gesture toward circulation itself—"flows, pipelines"—before ratcheting up the whole amalgam of poetry, nature, and economy with the poem's critical repetition of "slow":

Thru which the silence, too,
Has slowed, tho it's still refining
— me, I'm down to pre-war levels.

Here, the poem might suggest that the inaudibility associated with lyric poetry—an opacity not unlike Zukofsky's "upper register music" or Rimbaud's "departure for new noise"—whose refinements & corruptions, which in the end may not be all that different and which result in a kind of sublimation on the one hand and a kind of entropy on the other, that this silence has somehow "slowed." But what has it slowed? Or has this silence rather only "slowed-down," in the sense of having become less frequent, less available, less accessible, as if more & more of what remains to be heard—*the unknown*—were now somehow audible? Another delusion. But whereas "slowed" is actively voiced in the first tercet, the verb becomes ambiguously passive here in the third. It's unclear what is *doing* the slowing, I mean, what has "slowed" silence down? The high-speed networks of communications? The compressed channels of circulation, which reduce noise to information? Or maybe, in what would be a welcome reversal, "the silence"—or the poem—can be said to slow communication, the way it slows the flow of language otherwise pressed to serve as a lubricant to production. Would that poetry were able to claim something of a resistant force by refusing to communicate thru the same "flows, pipelines" that transport the equally and oppositely refined stuff of news & data! What other channels are there? Or is this resistance itself somehow slowing down, the way "wetlands and marshes" as a resistant barrier is both "slowing down" in the sense of becoming weakened, attenuated—like poetry—while still slowing down the pace of erosion? But "the silence" can just as readily refer to a failure to respond in a state of emergency, the sort of silence that we once said "equals death." In any case, "the silence" fails to reach us—be it the sublimed fumes of refined poetry, or the entropic noise of deregulated music—even as this silence moves thru the same channels as other so-called natural products—oil, gas, water—all of which have been pressed into the service of private networks—*not secret communications!*—the way information moves thru telecom grids and fiber cables. But maybe it's simply just to say: We can't afford refinement now, so this, the silence, my poem, sucks.

I hope this is good enough for you. At the very least, the little gauntlet you've run me thru has shown me how a poem might theorize itself "in its very praxis"—by way of its own prosody—a proposition I often repeat, but haven't managed to substantiate until now, in part because it can only happen in the poem itself and in ways that will always exceed my capacity to interpret. I mean, my understanding of what this poem is doing came after the fact of its composition. I didn't go into it thinking any of these things. Anyway, I began this letter really upset with you, but now I gotta thank you for giving me the opportunity to hear my poem as if for the first time.

Oh, and yeah, I'll leave the final line to yr imagination.

Now that you've managed to get this outa me, you'd better respond!

Love,
~ R.

MAIMED WELLBEING

A Somatic Exercise after CA Conrad

Perhaps you have loved someone who's been maimed or injured in one of America's ongoing wars. Perhaps you have cared for a Pakistani amputee who lost their limbs to an unmanned US drone. Perhaps you have assisted someone learning to walk with prosthetic legs, or who's had their organs removed or replaced as a result of a roadside bomb or IED. This is for *them*:

I'd been feeling the uncanny presence of spectral relations without knowing who or where my real relations are because they fall under the sign of "stranger," strangers with whom I am related thru circuits of exchange—money, goods, arms—these being the networks by which our intimacies are supported, the fabric of our social living. I'm referring to Iraqi women & Afghani men, Gazan boys & Pakistani girls lost in the debris of suicide bombs, missile attacks, or drone strikes executed with hardware produced down the road from where I live, or with the help of R&D funded by my IRA, and whose channels of circulation are the same channels thru which the means of my subsistence—food & clothing—travel, networks of goods that secure whatever material wellbeing I might call my own but whose own-ness shares a logic of ownership that informs the perishable corpse.

And yet, these relations—my relations, real relations—appear as though absolutely distant from me, so distant that to propose them as relations can only seem exaggerated, like an amplification whose sentiment bloats the figure of a body. And though my so-called "security" hangs on the vulnerability of their real bodies, my body's distance from the corpse-making apparatus, the militarized economy that structures and informs my everyday life, can only be felt as an infinite distance, tenuous & obscure.

How might my writing, as an extension of my body, perceive these relations, otherwise so withdrawn & occulted?

With these questions in mind, I took off for the woods one afternoon in search of a hovel—a hut, or a cave, or a tent, or a lean-to—a sign of abandoned living, or ephemeral protection, or any trace of habitation that one often encounters while hiking and that leaves a mysterious impression of life lived, or having been lived, in a way removed from my own. With this motive orienting my attention, I sat by the bank of a stream, took out my notebook and wrote without ceasing for 30 minutes. The next day, I took myself to a corner of the city, beneath the highway onramp, where homeless men and women live in elaborately built cardboard structures. I found a pot to sit on. The ground was damp, perhaps by urine, perhaps by beer, or a bit of water used for rinsing. This seemed like the right spot, so I took out my notebook and followed these instructions that I had prepared for myself in advance:

Imagine an architectural structure. Any building or designed social space will do. Now imagine an organ from within yr own body. This organ might be vital, like a lung, or sensory, like the skin, or reproductive, like an ovary. Place yr organ at the center of the architectural space as you imagine it. Align the position of yr organ so that a north/south axis runs thru it, and so the magnetic field oriented around northerly and southerly exposures within that architectural space is just barely disturbed by the presence of yr organ. This slight disturbance in the electromagnetic field is critical, so do not proceed until you are able, by virtue of the chosen organ, to sense, however subtly, this minimal rift, ripple, or fold in the social surround. Allow yr organ to conduct, communicate, or channel sensory impressions. Note how the architecture stabilizes or destabilizes the stream of unprocessed information. Note how yr organ is conducting, and whether the impressions are registering on its surface or in its depths. Now imagine a limb from the body of a recent war zone casualty suddenly situated in the same space as yr organ. Record, with copious detail, the disturbance this limb creates in yr imagined space, and whatever shifts in feeling & perception that ensue.

Now go home. From all the material gathered, score yr poem.

OFTEN I PISS ON THE NAMES OF FLOWERS

In shadows of the wound the camp
Engulfs embalmed platonic cock
And this is a way of ensuring castration
Will come to no extravagance

There being no secret language
Can hide nothing I mean to say
You better not believe the dead are not
Alive among us or I will die too

That's just a variant of something Notley
Writes in *Disobedience* "Or you will
Drown" and if you don't believe the dead
Are alive I mean if you believe the dead

Are deader than you then you ought to be
Dead yrself in their place motherfucker
For thou art dead asleep already

Their words throw light on this poem
The way yr organs do I mean

— *they emit a rosy glow*

THE ALGORITHM

In the event a detainee refrains from eating or drinking to the point where it is determined by medical assessment that continued fasting will result in a threat to life or seriously jeopardize health and involuntary feeling is required no direct action will be taken without the knowledge and written approval of the JTF-GTMO Commander. If the JTF-GTMO Commander makes the decision to authorize involuntary feeling of a detainee he/she will immediately inform the Commander United States Southern Command of his/her decision. In turn the Commander will notify appropriate Joint Staff and Department of Defense office of the necessity of initiating involuntary feeling of a detainee. This approval authority does not preclude the Medical Officer from performing any emergency actions deemed medically necessary to preserve life and health. Once a detainee on hunger strike meets the criteria for enteral feeling the following protocol may be initiated. After initial IV fluid resuscitation a medically cleared detainee may have treatment initiated with intermittent enteral feeling. In the event of a mass hunger strike isolating hunger-striking patients from each other is vital to prevent them from achieving solidarity. Given the inability to isolate patients in the DH because of the physical structure of the building initial IV fluid resuscitation lasting approximately 24 hours can occur in the DH followed by transfer back to Camp 5 to begin enteral feeling in an environment of single cell operation. Hospital Day #1: Vital signs should be checked at admission and every four hours for the first eight hours. If not drawn in the past two days a complete blood count (CBC) basic metabolic panel calcium magnesium phosphorus and creatine kinase should be obtained. A blood glucose reading (finger stick) should be documented in the Medication Administration Record. A 12 lead EKG will be performed upon admit. The detainee's admission weight should be recorded with weights being recorded daily thereafter. Fluid resuscitation should begin with a 1-2 liter bolus of normal saline. The amount of the IV bolus will be decided after reviewing the detainee's medical history for any co-morbid diseases. Thiamine 100mg IV one time. Give prior to giving dextrose of D5. This should be followed by a standard formulation which consists of one liter of D5 ½ normal saline with 20 mEq KCL one vial MVI 500 mg of magnesium sulfate one vial of trace elements and 1 mg of folic acid. This IV formulation should be run @ 100 ml/hr for 10 hours. Once the formulation has infused maintenance of fluids in the form of D5 ½ normal saline with 20 mEq KCL @ 100ml.hr should be started and continued until at least 48 hours after admission (Hospital Day #3). PRN medications during Phase 1: Glucose 50 grams IV if blood sugar < 60 and detainee lethargic or unresponsive. Tylenol 650 mg for pain headache. Mylanta 15-30 ml for indigestion heartburn. Initiation of Enteral Nutrition: Days #2 and #3. Place a 10 French r 12 French feeling tube into the patient's stomach per standard medical practice. Viscous lidocaine should be offered for the nostril and the throat. The tube should be well-lubricated prior to insertion. A linguist shall be present to assist with instructions. Once the feeling tube has been inserted the placement needs to be confirmed. This confirmation can be achieved by a standard chest x-ray or by air insufflation followed by a 10 ml test dose of water. The patient's head of the bed should be elevated at least 30-45 degrees while recumbent. A blood glucose level (via finger stick) should be documented every 12 hours X 3. The following labs should be considered on a daily basis for the initial 3-5 days beginning enteral feeling when the patient is at the high risk for re-feeling syndrome): basic metabolic panel calcium magnesium phosphorus ALT total bilirubin amylase albumin. Vital signs can be changed (if patient is stable). If clinically indicated continuous infusion of enteral feeling is initiated. Intermittent enteral feeds are performed under physician and nurse supervision. If the medical condition of the detainee requires closer observation he will be kept in the Detention Hospital. On feeling block medical staff closely monitors weight laboratory tests and general health of enterally felt detainees and evaluates and treats any side effects or complications of hunger striking. Involuntary enteral feeling shall be discontinued for detainees who have attained a calculated Ideal Body Weight (IBW) of 100% for fourteen (14) or more consecutive days of enteral feeling provided that an attending physician deems this medically acceptable. When detainee begins to eat voluntarily or after he is removed from enteral feeling based on 14 consecutive days of 100% IBW he is observed closed for re-feeling syndrome or food tolerance. Begin oral feelings with a bland diet and advance as tolerated to a regular diet. After having sufficient caloric intake for 3 days the detainee is removed from the hunger strike list and transferred to an observation block for further monitoring (approximately nine additional meals). Detainee is returned to normal detainee population. A physical evaluation is performed within 2 weeks of removal from hunger strike list. Detainee's weight and physical condition is monitored closely for 90 days followed by routine checks.

"The Algorithm" transcribes an excerpt from the Standard Operating Procedure: Medical Management of Detainees on Hunger Strike (SOP JTF-JMG #001 05 March 2013) exposed by Al Jazeera on 13 May 2013.

AFTER THE PRISON
following Rimbaud

When the idea of detention fails to keep us from the secret of our unhappiness, everyone's organs will revive in the halogen fog of creameries, merging dreams of care & waste. There'll be fossils for gathering lichens and utensils will invent new feasts! Lilies will awaken in the debris of San Quentin, as once tortured wounds withdraw now swollen with hypertrophic music. Out on the beaches, not much will have changed, but everything will be different.

Orchestrated sails dredge the bay for pearls as trade is reborn along avenues & quays. Shipping lanes careen with mussels from Juno & marbles from Macau, crude images from the Gulf & leafy greens from Calcutta. These figures soar emblazoned as sky becomes screen for a scene as opaque as Godard's last montage, source of stony vision. Plasma streams across the Northern Lights, whose reflections amp-up in melting ice. Cries blow thru theaters in Berlin. Children play in the ruins of Aleppo. Kids hide from death in a trench around Mosul as we conjure stained pictures of parties in Troy, where Hecuba's howl transfigures garlands of cinder & glass. Copper wire & fiber cable arouse habitations between LA and Shanghai. Scholars knit. Farmers write. Poets mint windings in the shadows of geese. People assemble to sing of moneyless morrows. Limbs find new form under xylophonic bulbs, as boys defuse in Cyprian nite. Now there's a Wurlitzter in the city square whose keys correspond to architectures free of constables & cops, a music to abolish Gaol! And the Safe House Belleville opens its doors beneath the neon mud of Guantánamo Bay.

Ever since, we listen to molten obsidian & Venusian shale, having closed our ears to men and their colonies of ants & drones. We invent new strains of arctic thyme hitherto unfathomed in song. Quince and cherries blossom in the saturated TV blue, having overcome the static & haze of trade wars. We wake to rumors of time's fulfillment—no suspension of seasons!—and say *no!* to sordid Tang. Ecumenical roulette summons Ponderosas on Lesbos! Organs and éclairs pass thru the Pacific's plastic vortex, untouched by maelstrom. Seas rise on a desert of toner. Light returns like Buffy from the grave denuding the camp of remaining shrubs, whose paw paws are cooler than Qaddafi back in '68.

Having minimized distance between the body & its conditions, our sadness becomes exquisitely insufferable, as stones turn to shell and shell to seed, transporting desire across terrestrial film, while the mystified reign of scarcity ignites this medicinal pottage to cure us of all we know

THE WOUND & THE CAMP, or VISCERAL SOLIDARITY
Some Notes toward a Radical Queer Poetics

What are the things that get in the way of care?
Why have you come back here, only to go away again?
Are some of the reasons hurtful but necessary?
— Oki Sogumi

This is how we were swept up by love,
we would say, and our arms were being
broken like shreds in those pieces of wood
— Raul Zurita

I felt a blanket put over me, though very thin, it comforted me.
— Mohamedou Ould Slahi

So when I write of love I write of
Binding referendums, bankruptcy intent,
Industrials, utilities and sales
The petitions of a citizens' group
Transportation, births, corrections
— Bernadette Mayer

1.0 Often I find myself thinking about the relation between private life and state violence, while wondering whether it's within poetry's reach to make the links between them perceptible by risking things both intimate and obscene.

1.1 My question hangs on the recognition that even the most personal of recessed intimacies (say, caretaking, masturbation & fucking) are penetrated by the most political of exposed systems (say, credit, wage & war). If in need of a formula, one might say: Immediate touch is mediated by abstract process; or, My most intimate being lies outside me.

2.0 I want a poetry that is inseparable from the body understood as a geopolitical situation or problem, but this is not the only thing poetry should or could be.

2.1 This is something I've tried to enact, with varying degrees of success and failure. In *Music for Porn*, I situate my body in relation to the body of a wounded US soldier in Afghanistan; while in *Common Place*, I do the same vis-à-vis a Yemeni man detained at Guantánamo Bay. The effort is to make distant and reified bodies—bodies reduced to things—proximate and intimate, while trying to make palpable the militarization that has captured our life-world.

2.2 I want to arouse the social relation between my body and certain "nonsites"—the soldier's wound & the detainee's cell, for example—where relation has become so abstract in its materialization that it seems to flicker on the horizon of its own negation, under siege by a ubiquitous militarism that penetrates every segment of our everyday lives.

2.3 Like the commodity, which similarly challenges my ability to feel the relations that shape the world, the nonsite can be both commonplace *and* exceptional, material *and* phantasmatic: "a sensuous thing which is at the same time supersensory" (Marx).

2.4 The Nonsite Collective adapted Robert Smithson's concept in its "Draft Proposal" in a way that I still find useful: "Nonsites may be scenes of transport in the sometimes unnavigable space between real social disasters and our critical apprehension of them." In other words, nonsites allow occulted geopolitical dynamics to become perceptible in their abstraction, like a negative imprint of some utopian desire for a common place.

2.5 As nonsites, both "soldier's wound" and "detention camp" risk mocking the very things they denote, which are much less "things" than processes whose intractable dynamics and effects are as multidimensional as the world and can only resist flat representation.

2.6 Put yet another way: "the wound" and "the camp" float away detached from the forces that make them. They are at the same time holes in militarized sense *and* common places born of property's circulation (arms, oil, or whatever) and always at the expense of very specific bodies. These are figures subject to flattened generalization: "the soldier," "the detainee," allegorical figures that could be replaced or joined by any number of others—"the illegal immigrant," "the convict"—assuming strange shapes around the abstract relations *obscene intimacies* that make our world.

2.7 Perhaps a poem can be a nonsite, too, making these figures felt thru the relations they obscure. I want to hazard this as a precondition for embodied thought.

3.0 All of this has as much to do with the banalities of everyday life *prosodic tenor of the drone* as it has to do with what Jodi Dean refers to as our "communist horizon;" as much to do with the degraded body of the Gitmo detainee as it has to do with the black body murdered by police in the streets of Baltimore, Madison, Charleston, New York, Ferguson, Cleveland, Oakland; as much to do with a body slain in Peshwar by a US drone operative in Tucson as it has to do with the trans-body segregated inside solitary in a Michigan prison called Kinross; as much to do with the promise of community as it has to do with the state of exception that negates that promise, be it in a detention camp or in a city square.

3.1 The most recent spectacularization of racialized violence makes it ever more clear that "the camp" can only fail to denote the location of a geographically isolated "sovereign exception" when power's unchecked capacity is the norm in the streets of every American city.

4.0 Often I find myself asking if a poem can open a space wherein I might feel, as if for the first time, something concrete in relation to bodies radically unlike my own, bodies especially vulnerable to militarized violence—bodies maimed by drones or killed by police, picked-off at a border or gassed at a security fence—bodies whose connection to mine has been rendered utterly abstract & unutterably opaque, bodies with which I'm meant to feel no binding tie, perhaps nothing at all, save a decorous sympathy guarded by commonplace feelings or a prescribed pity policed by platitudes. What might it mean to concretize this feeling as a relation of solidarity?

4.1 Maybe what I want is to encounter this question, without taking anything about poetry or solidarity for granted. Or maybe I want to embody an impossible response. In any case, the effort is one to make the often intangible militarization of our social relations visceral, and to locate that by way of my own body.

5.0 When I jot down the phrase "visceral solidarity," I may be seeking a form of recognition grounded in my flesh while accepting that the barriers to recognition—of the so-called "other," and thus also of my self—might themselves be critical for nourishing a politicized alliance whose center of gravity is not my head's ideas but rather my body's senses, an alliance inseparable from a concrete social bond—be it with someone lying in the street just outside my door, or someone half-a-world away—so that when that bond is violated or negated, be it by imprisonment or death, I'll feel the surge of rage or grief.

5.1 The importance I want to ascribe to the body's senses in all this begs the question: How can a poem arouse those senses in a way that short-circuits whatever dominant regimes of representation have already organized them?

5.2 Can feelings of rage & grief be revolutionary? I'm not sure. But I do think they're bound up with visceral solidarities across otherwise unbridgeable divides, solidarities without which revolutions can't adequately imagine themselves into being.

5.3 In the interest of that imagination, I want to render situations that betray codified forms of empathy, situations where feelings of compassion for violently othered bodies might be impeded or blocked. It's the contradictions obscured by familiar temptations to identify or empathize that a poem might arouse: a form of rage or grief and that resists its own consolations.

5.4 Given that the obstacles to these feelings often seem insurmountable, they might require an improbable fantasy of relation. For me, such a fantasy would likely assume an erotic dimension as the visceral organizes itself around the most sensitive of physical arousals, an affirmation of connection whose passion may move inside the fear of love, which is also the fear of failing to love.

5.5 These fears took shape in my adult life in ways inseparable from the HIV-related crises of the 1980s.

6.0 I've never lost sight of my apprenticeship to queer art in its struggle to respond to AIDS when an artwork might have had to refuse everything "proper" about mourning, everything quiet, distant, ideal, abstract—to the point even of refusing the common sense of sympathy and compassion, whose norms often sadly serve to stabilize the status quo—in order to politicize loss under violent conditions determined to neutralize it: Throwing a beloved's ashes on the White House lawn vs. Quilting panels on the Mall. So maybe this has been about the struggle to mourn all along.

6.1 In a recent email exchange, my friend Earl Jackson reminded me of the sea-change in queer desire that occurred during the late 1980s thru the mid-1990s with the advent of AOL chat-rooms, cam sites & bulletin boards, and how these "new erotic zones" spectacularized a kind of distance for intimate ends and mutual care, allowing one to gaze at the body of the other far removed from potentially deadly contact. "People could see each other naked," Earl writes, "and each person's self-pleasuring was ricocheted back to the subject as the spectacle got another person off. This was a multi-phasic response to the plague—one saw the body that was too far away to touch, but that distance became the conduit of desire." This is one way in which the space between bodies who might never touch became newly charged with erotic promise.

6.2 I never availed myself of any of the sites Earl mentions, although I once flirted with phone sex in the early 1990s when flashy toll numbers would regularly appear bannered across the pages of every weekly fag rag capturing customers with a model's predictable straight-boy looks, stimulating pleasure's migration from the eye to the ear. But, while turned on by the prospect, I always hung-up before uttering a word.

6.3 Wasn't it Sade who referred to the ear as the most erotic of organs? The orifice penetrated by word & voice, narration & song.

6.4 Improbably, I'm reminded here of Jean de Léry's sixteenth-century stay among the Tupinamba recorded in *The History of a Voyage to the Land of Brazil, Also Called America* (1578) as Léry was drawn by way of his ear to a hut where the Tupi males were chanting and dancing: "At the beginning of the ritual, I was in the women's house," he writes, and continues, "I had been somewhat afraid, but then received in recompense such joy, hearing the measured harmonies of such a multitude, and especially the cadence and refrain of the song. I stood there transported by delight. Whenever I remember it, my heart trembles, and it seems their voices are still in my ears." It's a primal scene of dual penetrations: Léry pierces the thatch of the hut so that he might see the bodies lost in ceremony, and in turn he's pierced by the otherness of song, as an auditory hallucination becomes inseparable from one's own ear.

6.5 I can still hear the decaying note of Léry's narration traversing centuries and contexts when I read Samuel R. Delany's narration of his revelatory moment at the St. Mark's Baths, circa 1963—an inversive complement of Léry's encounter—as Delany penetrates the gym replete with an "undulating mass of naked male bodies spread wall-to-wall," a scene pregnant with a future of somatic plenitude and political power. "My first response was a kind of heart-thudding astonishment," he writes. "Whether male, female, working or middle class, the first direct sense of political power comes from the apprehension of massed bodies. That I'd felt it and was frightened by it meant that others had felt it too. [...] I was afraid, but I moved forward into it." This is how an understanding of oneself as a social body critically connected to the bodies of others emerges from the vertiginous space between what can be sensed and what can be said, between the visible and the speakable.

6.6 Perhaps what I am calling "visceral solidarity" emerges thru—with and between—these related scenes of encounter, identification & difference, scenes at once similar & opposed, wedded & antithetical.

6.7 In stark contrast to Delany's narration, Léry erases the very thing he desires, founding & grounding a new sense of self, the so-called "subject of European humanism," by writing his voyeuristic encounter with the indigenous other. As Michel de Certeau remarks, this is a scene of inauguration & initiation, where one's witnessing *surveilling* the native body yields the "'savage' page on which Western desire will be written." Once that body does its work to produce the metaphysics of European personhood, it becomes a repository *grave* for the culture's imaginary refuse.

6.8 This is also a scene of endlessly productive loss, as the European self is founded on what is forever banished from it, and the writer's identification with that loss becomes endlessly generative of more writing.

6.9 One challenge for poetry committed to visceral solidarity would be to find a form whereby one might "cradle the body always not 'here,'" as Earl puts it, demystifying an absence without disavowing that one is only cradling oneself. Can a poem be such a form without becoming another guilty pleasure that creates the body it then bears witness to, fantasizing and expelling the thing it requires, and only then desires, in the interest of authorizing an isolated scene that mirrors rather than refutes the dynamics of power it would like to imagine itself refusing?

7.0 In any case, poetry is not activism. While it can sing against social violence in its many guises, its semantic consolations and sonic reverb are no corrective for injustice & oppression. That said, poetry can arouse a utopian desire, a stimulant for radical fantasy & visceral solidarity, adding to the gut flora that nourishes resistance, enabling us to feel our relations to real conditions without resolution, while moving our bodies toward the bodies of others struggling against these conditions, in streets, squares, and prisons.

7.1 Especially inside the prison, against all institutional expectations and constraints, I've learned that "poetry" can become a scene of study, an "undercommons" (Moten and Harney), or a "concrete utopia" (Bloch), both of which nourish alternative futures as they emerge together with a critical consciousness determined to abolish its own conditions.

7.2 Inside the prison, poetry can work like a canopy undercover of which fugitive things might happen, turning otherwise negated forms of social connection into the stuff of living communion, producing new ways of knowing and acting, while constructing unforeseen horizons of social promise even under asocial conditions. This has everything to do with how poetry is able to provide a place to gather, enabling forms of agency and self-organization, collective study and mutual aid, while cultivating a deeply rooted—that is, radical—sense of empowerment, even inside the disempowering environment of the carceral system.

7.3 At the same time, the practice of poetry inside the prison makes our understanding painfully clear that the channels and institutions thru which poetry moves are governed and policed by the very logics poetry might take aim to disrupt.

8.0 While all these propositions and questions may seem to advocate for a certain ethics, there exists no ethical stance for poetry that is not itself caught up in violent dynamics and processes outside of which poetry might wish hygienically to imagine itself.

8.1 Like poetry, ethics arguably manifests an idealist discourse, a philosophical consolation—"the mists of ethics," Genet called it—but there's no ethical view from nowhere that isn't the view of a specific body caught in the grip of the grid.

8.2 I don't want this to be confused with a familiar call for acknowledging "complicity" in one's poetry. That's too easy a reflex. Why should we need a poem to remind us of what is most obvious? ("The awful presence of the obvious," Bernadette Mayer calls it.) Rather: What can a poem make perceptible about my body's relation to socially sanctioned violence that I don't already know or feel? And what about the unacknowledged contradictions that every insistence on the ethical obscures?

8.3 Put still another way: Poetry's sentimental belief in its ethical responsibility, like its traditional claim for empathy or its invitation to identify, always risks becoming an extension of liberal democracy's humanitarian paternalism, which sees itself as a promising liberator of admissible forms of suffering life, as if any such liberation wouldn't first necessitate liberal democracy's own overcoming. And what about those forms of life that fail the admissions test?

8.4 Whereas the discourse around ethics is often one of idealism, at once disembodied and consoling, the language organized by poetry can be charged to refuse these comforts while still arousing pleasure, being at once embodied, discomfiting, & prosodic.

8.5 It's been said that ethics can only be lived as a refusal to reproduce the terms of its own unethical conditions. Without experiencing that refusal as loss, I want a poetry that can tease out a dialectics of refusal at the heart of whatever effort to refuse if only to make the obstructions to that refusal palpable.

9.0 Unlike melancholy—my obstinate attachment to loss to the point of identifying with it—mourning can transform life affirmatively, embodying loss without becoming it. But as Denise Riley insists, "to get that distinction clear, just for yourself, will demand a forensic labor" (*Time Lived Without Its Flow*). Riley immediately qualifies her proposition, urging one (herself) to assess "one's responsibility in the death" in a way that "needn't entail your masochism." I'm moved by this notion of a "forensic labor" and by the critical-aesthetic practice it suggests.

10.1 For radical photographer Allan Sekula, "forensic methods (detective methods focusing on evidence and the body) offer a tool for oppressive states, but forensic methods have also become tools of opposition."

10.2 "Forensic" has its etymological root in the "forum," a social space for the production of public knowledge and antagonistic discussions of legal, political and economic questions. But insofar as it's been shaped by the needs of the court—*surveillance & police*—forensics becomes yet another adjunct to the violent ends of law, and while it wants to transcend the instability of human testimony, forensics can never exceed the subjectivity it denies.

10.3 The poetics of stealing the forensic language produced by the state might require extravagant forms—an equal and opposite overkill—in order to counter the excesses of violence responsible for negating our real social relations to the detained & murdered. The poem born of such a poetics might aim to wrest the stuff of public knowledge away from the apparatuses of power that produce and press such knowledge to carceral ends: detention, imprisonment, deportation, disappearance. Following Sekula, I'll call such *détourned* knowledge "counter-forensic."

11.0 "What is forensics," asks Gertrude Stein in the concluding pages of *How To Write*, and she answers without pause, "forensics is an argument to be fought." Forensics is "a master piece of strategy," she goes on, "an argument of their deliberation. The forensics of abuse which has not been written." For Stein, forensics is language's own alibi to cover-up an abuse that can't be named as such. "Forensics is in the state," she writes. Insofar as her entire body of work constitutes a commitment to making this abuse an open secret thru her own sustained pathology report on language itself, a kind of linguistic post-mortem, Stein is a pioneer of the "counter-forensics" I want to pursue.

12.0 In its encounter with the linguistic traces of material force (i.e., autopsy report, prison record, court confession, police interrogation, tribunal sentence), a counter-forensic poetic practice would aim to radicalize the subjectivity that so-called forensic-science disavows, to embody relation at the limit of valued relation if only to feel those relations and think those limits as if for the first time.

12.1 My approach to counter-forensics wants to arouse a sensuous intimacy at the place where that intimacy has become distant and intangible, say, in the language of "evidence" in which real bodies are replaced by real abstractions. No longer needed, they languish and sublime as surplus or waste.

12.2 At the same time, a counter-forensic poetry might name a strategy for transporting illicit materials *wrong knowledge* across the borders of policed institutions and disciplined forms. Like other fugitive poetries, it refuses to reproduce its own assumptions & values. Rather, counter-forensics names a set of practices that declines to countenance its own self-disciplining aims: Poetry as the sign of a discipline whose wager is its own undoing. Poetry as anti-discipline. Poetry as unwelcomed interloper. Poetry as trafficker. Poetry as contraband. Poetry as the impossible. Poetry as misbegotten & ungovernable. Poetry as thief of ice & fire.

13.0 But what happens when the only thing a poem can steal is the evidentiary language denoting the body whose trauma it claims to document? What place does the writer's body occupy as an active agent in the mediation of that language and the reproduction of its conditions? Imagine a Bartleby who refuses and copies *at the same time*, performing what I call "metabolic transcription" wherein body & document collide. What might it mean to attend to the elisions in that collision?

13.1 So when masturbation fails, I work
Transcribing autopsy reports because I want to
Merge with you and in merging become not one
The way the myth assures but infinitely limited as

I fulfill
The promise of my individual person in this infinity
Of military hardware & online shopping whose auto
- nomous value informs my inner life, illuminates
The body viewed thru a cell window where he lay
Not breathing. Reported to be in that fetal position
Covered with a blanket, head slightly tilted, hands
& feet exposed when the guards enter to secure a
Decedent's swollen tongue, I notice the defining
Thing, a ligature consisting of an elastic band tightly
Wrapped at least twice around his neck, twisted
On the left, having to be cut from the same. At approx
- imately 2200 hours he asks for a nurse, requests a sleep
- ing pill and is last known alive 10-15 minutes later
When he calls for the guard to close his 'bean hole
Cover,' a sign meaning he's ready to sleep. A few
Minutes later he's discovered unmoved & unresp
- onsive. That's when I enter to sponge his brow
Before wrapping the ligature around my cock secur
- ing the thing at the base of my balls where the press
- ure keeps me hard as I caress his head on my thigh
Close my eyes and sing.
Because unlike 'a clerk
Cataloging the results of a premise' (that's Sol LeWitt)
I admit libidinal impulses otherwise subtracted from
The record, like extraneous sensations, the real smell
Of rectal mucus, my organs touching the social limit
His body, 'blunt indefatigable fact' (that's Sylvia Plath)
If only to pit report against its administration
Stifle the sound of autopsy's universal tongue
By including swollen things outside the image or be-
- yond the imaginable like someone's shiver in Sade
Whose perversion is nothing but an empty place

In the order of property an unspeakable name
That is no name and will never be proper and whose
Dirtiness makes it common or whose banality
Makes it sleazy like Justine's shudder banned the way
A fake name exceeds obligation to service virtue
- 's four detained boys in succession as they tie me
With strings attached to every part and pull at will
And I sway & lose balance on the edge of losing my
Self the way they introduce stones & pipes to each
Hole whose emptiness opens on unthinkable pleasure
The way exuberance destroys the one who narrates
It there being no common subject as all human me
- asure dissolves, withdrawn inside his cell.

13.2 While the prosodic pleasures of the poem allow me to sense a relation at the site of relation's negation, pleasure, like eros, has a gendered & racialized history with which my feelings are enmeshed. At best, the poem's music might attune itself to these histories, help make them audible, even if this means the undoing of the lyric subject, an undoing that requires lyric.

13.3 As Jessica Benjamin writes, "a politics that cannot cope with contradiction, that denies the irrational, that tries to sanitize the erotic, fantastic components of human life cannot visualize an authentic end to domination but only vacate the field." I want a poetry that contributes to the difficult work of feeling the irrational contradictions and erotic fantasies that both inform the field and lubricate the means to overturn its crappy soil.

14.0 Like a "philosopher of the feel" (Moten & Harney), a poem can sense what can't be contained by dominant frames of recognition—the inadmissible & incongruous—an excess that can't yet be named, vehicle to another *where* that's always already *here*. Put another way:

A poem is a critical organ of sensation, a prosthetic extension of the body capable of sensing the active non-existence of the world we've failed to make.

14.1 Like utopian desire, such a poem is penetrated by the very conditions it longs to overcome, conditions whose transformation would make the poem irrelevant. Even if such a poem can only fail to supersede the limits it endeavors to feel, it can still move us toward the obstructions—at once material & imagined, concrete & abstract—that block the world we long to make if only as a prelude to sensing another world beyond them.

15.0 *Let this be the Body / through which the War has passed.* Solmaz Sharif quotes these lines of Frank Bidart's in her book called *Look*, a remarkable collection that also lifts and turns phrases from the *Department of Defense Dictionary of Military and Associated Terms* in poems that transform the violence of euphemized war-speak into the language of tenderness, intimacy & care. Bidart's long poem from which the lines derive, "The War of Vaslav Nijinsky," actually repels me with its sexual guilt, but I love the lines Sharif quotes once they are detached from the poem's reproach. This helps me to understand that my own poems can only bear witness to the distance between my body and the wars, a distance that often feels total but is as close as the most intimate caress.

15.1 In its effort to embody the otherwise abstract violence of our militarized world, a poem might default to erotic fantasy in order to arouse a visceral relation to the fallen & detained, a relation whose concrete irreality can be allegorized thru the language of sex—*false immediacy of erotic touch*—to enable a reader to feel something otherwise banished from perception.

15.2 What I mean by the erotic here is no gratuitously amped-up trope, but a poetical figure that makes it possible to imagine a relation whereby touch could become the scene of visceral care rather than violent harm. But a lot hangs on that "could," as the desire for the one is inseparable from the risk of the other.

15.3 No doubt, the language of sexuality is a fully processed and codified language, one that reproduces a logic of domination precisely at the moment when it would have us believe—recalling Michel Foucault's famous expression—that our liberation from power is in the balance.

15.4 Often I find myself thinking about how, despite its codification, the discourse of sexuality might inform a poetics—call it post-pornographic—that promises in some small way to expose my body, if only to language, making it vulnerable enough to imagine relations and intimacies against the grain of dominant common sense.

15.5 If systems of domination and exploitation are continually reproduced in the social relations that comprise our everyday lives, how might we begin to imagine those relations differently without forgetting that our efforts to resist move within the very same language and logics those efforts aim to disrupt and transform? What's the use of a militant queer art if not to make these tensions and contradictions perceptible?

15.6 I suppose I want to remain faithful to the end of *The History of Sexuality*, which proposes "a different economy of bodies and pleasures" whereby Foucault anticipates, without prescribing, another form of social reproduction, another way of organizing, living and feeling the relations between bodies, one that will have superseded, I like to think, the current system of value and its violent depredations. Ultimately, this will require the movement beyond sexuality itself.

And yet, the current economic order of things—inseparable from military order—cleaves to sex as it is currently lived.

15.7 For all these reasons, I find myself longing for a poem that can attune my senses and orient my desires to the promise of another economy—or perhaps no economy!—where bodies and pleasures will be experienced in a radically different way, even if the only thing such a poem might make perceptible are the obstacles to the transformed conditions it longs for, obstacles of which the poem itself is an extension.

16.0 I suppose I want to run right into what Judith Butler calls "the nexus of violence and sexuality" at the heart of the so-called "civilizing mission" by inhabiting rather than disavowing that nexus and, in doing so, to risk turning the scene of conditioned aggression into one of unconditioned love, to wrest some form of solidarity—*irreducibly visceral*—away from the forces that aim to eliminate even the idea of such solidarity, that is, to force a frame within which that solidarity might appear against the force whose power repudiates its possibility.

16.1 Can a poem dramatize an otherwise inadmissible form of alliance without reproducing the assumptions that abet the power of subjection to presumed identities, desires & beliefs?

16.2 When conceived in erotic fantasy, a poem can throw light on the limits of what's imaginable in its effort to feel something beyond those limits. What I call "radical fantasy" might allow you to feel the structures that obstruct the world you long to inhabit as part of the effort to build that world. Often I find myself desiring a poetry that can touch the horizon of this other world, without deluding myself that I am anywhere but here.

16.3 Fantasy, like poetry, is structured by the world it aims to move beyond. There's no fantasy exempt from this constraint. In this sense, fantasy is not a dreamer's dream, autonomous and unconstrained, but the means by which to feel one's unfreedom. This is not fantasy as escape, but rather as a flight *toward* the real.

17.0 "The wound" and "the camp" name sites, or nonsites, where every effort to represent my imaginary relations to real conditions—*bodies under siege*—is threatened both by the spectacle of visibility and the spectacle of absence: by kitsch, on the one hand, and prohibition, on the other.

17.1 There can be no imaginary resolution to these tensions & contradictions that isn't always immediately betrayed. Perhaps it's not the business of poetry to offer imaginary solutions to real contradictions, but rather to make the blocks to those solutions acutely palpable. One such block might be identification itself upon which other blocks are based: surveillance, policing, detention.

17.2 And so I long—*inconceivably*—to make myself unknown in this effort, if only to reciprocate an encounter with the other as other, and to ground love on the failure to identify.

18.0 While a love poem can never transcend the material conditions that constrain and frustrate it, it can make those conditions available to some of our strongest feelings in the interest of transforming them. As Andrea Brady writes: "Love is the determination to make a world, which requires us also to risk destroying one."

18.1 What I'm proposing may be nothing less than the most hackneyed notion of the love lyric, understood *not* as individual expression but as the concretization of a so-called "universal experience"—say, the extraction of our most personal feelings for corporate ends, or the reification of our intimate relations, together with the refusal of all these alienations—as if, thru the amplified subjectivity of a degraded fantasy, I might at last touch its objective conditions, conditions frozen in military hardware & prison cells, container ships & cheap debt. How ludicrous would it be to claim that a poem might want this and only this, even if the horizon of such a poem can only be the dissolution of its own possibility?

18.2

You are my common name
But it could be anyone's
And if yr body is not

Even yrs to love you meaning
- fully can only mean
To risk what I am

The loving solution being this

— *dissolution of the lover.*

19.0 Still, I wonder if a poem can arouse the intimacy it longs for when the conditions of that intimacy have been violently abstracted, mediated, distanced? Turned inside out, the question is: Can a poem help us to imagine *what is*, that is, to imagine what we ought not to have to imagine? If so, this would be a poem that materializes a nonsite, or a non-synchronous space between sensual experience and abstract process, the place of my displacement.

19.1 And so, I find myself imagining the poem as if it were a phantom limb with bodily intensity, tuning my whole organism to respond to conditions I can't fully grasp even as I act within them. Maybe this is the poem's urgent response-ability.

20.0 The only world we hold in common may be the one that doesn't yet exist. And while we may all share the preconditions of this other world, we share them in radically different ways (i.e., the uneven distribution of comfort and precarity, what Danny Hayward calls "the excess of our unfulfillment"). How then are we to imagine life held in common across the most radically diverse spaces of our social world—from cozy bed to prison cot—where solidarities might seem inconceivable without falling for the lures of guilt, complicity, despair? How might a poem feel this common life while simultaneously registering the obstructions blocking its transformation?

20.1 All these notes open on an endless cascade of other questions: How to cultivate a poetics that challenges the immunities upon which political sovereignty and its military violence hang harnessed to legal personhood & profit, individual identity & property? What might it mean for the poem to imagine forms of vulnerability & care that are critical for a countervailing communion? Can a poem help us to anticipate, embody and enact unthinkable solidarities in the interest of revolutionizing the conditions of our conditioned love?

20.2 While all of these questions only amount to an extravagant thought experiment, I'm longing for a poetry that can move me to its limits.

Works Consulted or Quoted:

Giorgio Agambem, *The State of Exception.* Jessica Benjamin, *The Bonds of Love: Psychoanalysis, Feminism, and the Problem of Domination.* Frank Bidart, "The War of Vaslav Nijinsky," in *The Sacrifice.* Ernst Bloch, *The Principle of Hope.* Andrea Brady, "The Determinations of Love." Judith Butler, *Frames of War.* Michel de Certeau, *The Writing of History.* Douglas Crimp, "Mourning and Militancy." Jodi Dean, *The Communist Horizon.* Michel Foucault, *The History of Sexuality, volume 1.* Jean Genet, *Thief's Journal.* Earl Jackson, Jr., personal email correspondence. Stefano Harney & Fred Moten, *The Undercommons: Fugitive Planning & Black Study.* Danny Hayward, "Poetry and Self-Defense." Jean de Léry, *History of a Voyage to the Land of Brazil, Also Called America* (1578). Bernadette Mayer, *Midwinter Day.* The Nonsite Collective, "A Draft Proposal." Denise Riley, *Time Lived, Without Its Flow.* Allan Sekula, "Photography and the Limits of National Identity." Solmaz Sharif, *Look.* Mohamedou Ould Slahi, *Guantánamo Diary.* Robert Smithson, "Provisional Theory of Nonsites." Oki Sogumi, "The Longest Month." Gertrude Stein, *How to Write.* Eyal Weizman, "Introduction: Forensis." Alberto Toscano & Jeff Kinkle, *Cartographies of the Absolute.* Raul Zurita, "Colonia Dignidad Prison," in *The Country of Planks* (translated by Daniel Borzutsky).

MY AUGUSTINE
(a fragment)

— I didn't see the body. His body. Not that the sight always helps to anchor yr belief in the fact —

It's not the eyes, I wrote when I was sad, but the lids that close, behind which fakes the fire-fangled house, my pre-fab fold-up collapsible dupe-box, a single trick or concrete slab, a white-hot artifice or universal heap, this waste from which my love will be reborn. Someone can communicate the corpse, I say to myself, as if it's been here all along, but the missing evidence, yr withdrawn body, betrays my cause the way a thick squall befalls a thing now gone, erasing every trace. I wasn't there to hold you when you died, so I ate you, and now y've become me. This is how a song of myself becomes pure necromancy. I can't resemble you anymore, nor myself for that matter, and so my poem's unrecognizable. This whole thing amounts to what it feels like to breathe underwater, all the crustaceous debris, the shell and the bone, pieces of a broken kiss now dead. No paint can conceal such an aborted belief in nature, my poem, a sentient abscess where this sentence abandons me in yr name, a deposit lodged inside my thigh, or some pure mote in *dura mater*, a speck in the brain's grey matter, a line in a report that ought to have been yrs, the way a catheter ran from my hand to yr lung thru a hole the size of a lug in yr back as I sucked the fungus out, raw matter for my prosody, or some such semblance of a desert tent wherein I find myself again aroused, like I was that November afternoon in '94. We were in North Beach and I was lying beside you on the grass in Washington Square, yr body burning like a dozen suns so every organ burst in flames when you touched me, soon thereafter becoming stone. What I'm hoping to describe is the opposite of security under whose sign there can be no poetry, one's exposure to language being anything but safe. The event is geological and leaves a fossil record like a star, that "stone glowing" in Ceravolo's *Millenium Dust.* You were feeling the best you had in weeks, and what I felt felt more like love than anything I'd ever felt before. This line might bear yr impress or negation, a diluted memory whose words estrange my sense. Not long after that, they found me sprawled on white shag in yr underpants, but I convinced myself it wasn't really me. Snapshots ensued, more photos followed.

I'd been tagged inside a little lapse or spell, the image of them doing things with pliers, plastic tubes, forceps and glue, anything to provoke a state of sad awakening. Nothing can annul this period without end or suspend an endless contrivance, my story, a closed system of ash & sand crushed by anti-force, yr gelatinous waves keep coming when I no longer can. I never thought there'd come a moment when what would be would be you no longer here, reconstituted by lost objects, other bodies' haloed injuries, my love-pitched phantasies, not knowing how to grieve the passing of ripples to shore, the proper name itself a thing that drops like a pebble, sunk like a stone, it keeps things coming and they all keep coming back, evanescent pictures of my own disappearance, that silver chain you tied to lace. Yr words become my body's cover, a veil whose grace returns you. How will I survive this sadness with no disaster to explain it, you, a pronoun that devours, an inconsolable name, standing in for nothing, a sign my apparition produced while streaming toward a sudden discharge, as if the present had been haunted by you even then when you were here, the way architecture houses ruin, a form unfinished mourning takes when rubble is unthinkable. I don't know who you are and grow tired of telling myself the story. Scanning old dreams, I mistake yr ghost and stitch some bitching rents together. Each plot point's like a buttress flying, holding up the structure of whatever home we made to abandon. When you said you wanted to fuck me, I could feel yr ideas pushing deep into my bowels, but never you, yr lips unfathomed, hidden like flamingoes in the shrubs, the way they awaken signs of something else. I only want to burrow beneath the shadow of yr wings, by whose image I mean to refresh a gross affliction, but even wings conceal an allusion to power, a memory I've tried to escape and get no further than this sentence, like the one John Donne composed in a sermon: "For in this Metaphor of *Wings*, the Holy Ghost expresses the *Maritime* power, the power of Nations at Sea, in Navies (*Woe to the land shadowing with wings*) that hover over the world, and intimidates with sailes and ships." So I seek comfort and refreshment in the misery from which I seek deliverance, the way you go on living in my body from which this bird emerged, a form unfinished mourning takes, too big to contain itself entirely. This is how history turns us into freely floating feelings no one ever has, where I come to life, a perfect gas, or rhododendron, a word too wild to fit my mouth. Still, the best hiding place remains beneath my bed, too big to think it, the place you open to authorize me. My father insists something happened that night in the tub, running his finger along my fissure in white porcelain to prove the point, an untraceable fault, scarless along the rib, as if to say, "Look, no disruption, no separation," but I can't stop expanding with currents convulsive, they blister my mouth inside of which you've gone, the sore from which these lines emerge, my present tense contracting the way love contracts me to the future from whose point of view this will not have been terminal.

ACKNOWLEDGMENTS

Weak Link is an interstitial work. Everything collected here has been recovered from the faults and cracks within and between four books—*Rumored Place, Disaster Suites, Music for Porn* and *Common Place*—which together comprise one long serial work. No book can ever contain itself, so while these poems & essays have not been moored to any of the aforementioned titles, they remain integral to the larger canvass they exceed, while also suggesting a "weak link" to a current work-in-progress, *My Augustine*, a fragment of which concludes this volume.

Section epigraphs are adapted or quoted from the following: Robert Duncan, "The Structure of Rime V"; Leslie Scalapino's *Defoe*; V. I. Lenin, *What Is To Be Done?*; and Denise Riley, *Time Lived, Without Its Flow.*

"Hoax" first saw the light of day in *The Brooklyn Rail* with the title "Art of the Cover-Up: Gerhard Richter's *Decke* (1988)," and benefited from an early reading by Barrett Watten, who pointed me toward Robert Storr's excellent monograph on Richter's RAF sequence, entitled *October 1977.* Many thanks to my dear friend, Christian Sälzer, for his generous response to my query regarding the rich connotations of the word *Decke.*

"The Usufruct of the Land (Being No Solution to Crisis)" was first published in *The Poetic Front* (Vancouver 2010), edited by Stephen Collis, and contributes to my ongoing collaboration with Thom Donovan, entitled *Usufruct.*

"Literal Hallucination" was written specifically for "A Tonalist Poetry," edited by Laura Moriarty for *Jacket* 40.

"Theses on the Remembrance of Things to Come" continues a sequence begun in *Rumored Place* and borrows occasionally from Guy Debord's "Theses on the Paris Commune" and Leslie Scalapino's *Defoe*. This sequence was first published in *War and Peace 3/The Future*, co-edited by Leslie Scalapino and Judith Goldman. I dedicate the sequence here *in memoriam* to Leslie Scalapino.

"The Rhetoric of Blood" was guided by generous feedback from Robin Tremblay-McGaw and Melissa Buzzeo while it was in progress. Gratitude to Norma Cole for responding to its earliest draft.

"Pornotopias" collects notes originally prepared for my workshop at Naropa University's Summer Writing Program, called "Pornotopias" (June 2011), and more expansively presented as a talk for the Nonsite Collective (August 2011). Special thanks to Rich Owens for suggesting that I assemble this material for *Damn the Caesars: Crisis Inquiry*, where the text first appeared (Summer 2012). Section 12.0 is lifted from *Music for Porn*, with gratitude to Nightboat Books. It was hard for me to resist the temptation to revise this text extensively to better reflect more recent thinking. Had I done so, however, I would have had to reorganize this material from the ground up, taking as a new point of departure Hortense Spillers' notion of the "pornotrope" in "Mama's Baby, Papa's Maybe: An American Grammar Book," and Alexander Weheliye's critical elaboration of this concept in *Habeas Victus: Racializing Assemblages, Biopolitics and Black Feminist Theories of the Human.* Sadly, I was unaware of Spillers' work when I first assembled these notes.

The title sequence of poems, "Weak Link," was published as a chapbook by Slack Buddha Press (2009), with gratitude to publishers Bill and Lisa Howe. Selections from this sequence also appear in *[——] Placeholder*, published in the UK by Enitharmon (2016), as do "Prelude to Commodious," "This Cell in My Head," and "Essay on the Siege."

The poem that begins "Wetlands and marshes slow" appears in *Disaster Suites*, with gratitude to Jane Sprague and Palm Press. "Maimed Wellbeing" was written specifically in response to a prompt from Bhanu Kapil during a workshop at "Movement, Somatics and Writing: A Practice-Based Research Symposium" in Ann Arbor (February 2011), and was further developed in my class "Somatic Writing: Body, Language, Text" at Eastern Michigan University. "After the Prison," after Rimbaud's "Après le Deluge," was inspired by and written for the women in The Writers' Bloc, an ongoing poetry workshop that I facilitate at Women's Huron Valley Prison, Michigan.

"The Wound and the Camp" was written in response to a call for a "Post-Crisis Poetics" that ran in *Armed Cell* 10, edited by Brian Ang, and it originally appeared at postcrisispoetics.blogspot.com on 4/8/17. Many thanks to Carla Billitteri and her students in Documentary Poetics at University of Maine, Orono, for critical conversations around my notes when still in draft. I completed the text with further instigations & guidance from Alli Warren, Yosefa Raz, and Bruce Boone. Upon revising it for *Weak Link*, "The Wound and the Camp" benefited from an engagement at Michigan State University, where I presented a work-in-progress called "'Mute Opposable Evidence': or The Body/Poem as Witness and Opposition: Toward a Counter-Forensic Poetics for Abolition" for the Hyphens Lecture Series. Gratitude to Divya Victor. Several passages in "The Wound & the Camp" also figure as part of an essay entitled "Useless Commodities, Disposable Bodies: An Essay on Value and Waste," which appears in *Against Value in the Arts and Education*, edited by Ladkin, McKay, and Bojesen (2016). Sections 13.1 and 18.2 are lifted from *Common Place*, with gratitude to Ugly Duckling Presse.

A very early version of "My Augustine (A Fragment)" first appeared in *Harrington Gay Men's Fiction Quarterly* (1999) with the title "An Essay of Augustine." A longer version of this fragment is forthcoming in an anthology of queer poetry edited by Eric Sneathen, Sophie Robinson, and Joshua Jones (Boiler House Books, UK).

In addition to those already named, many thanks to the editors of the following for supporting some of the work included here: *West Wind Review, Abraham Lincoln, Hi Zero, Fanzine, Northern Ohio Review, New American Writing, Where Eagles Fly, Poem-A-Day* (Academy of American Poets), *Try!, Z"L* (for the family of CJ Martin and Julia Drescher), *Black Box Manifold*, and *Resist Much/Obey Little: Inaugural Poems to the Resistance.*

Many of these poems were written expressly for friends: "Lovers of Kairos," for David Brazil; "Prelude to Commodious" for Peter Linebaugh; "When you whispered the secret," for kari edwards; "Bird Crave," for Eirik Steinhoff; "Our Remains Unwritten," "A Cell in My Head," and "All Roof No House," were all written for Thom Donovan; "The Chill of Enclosure," for Amy Balkin; "Enthymeme," for Camille Roy; "How to Say 'Commons'" for Brian Teare and Frances Richard; "This Rock, No Place" for Brenda Iijima; "Barren Tender" for Taylor Brady; "After Mallarmé," a translation of "Le vierge, le vivace et le bel aujourd'hui," for Brandon Brown; and "Communion" for Blandine Paranque.

Infinite gratitude to Lyn Hejinian and Travis Ortiz for the opportunity to gather and organize my weak links; to Derek Fenner for designing this home for them; and to Dee Dee Kramer for gracing the cover with a remixed detail from "Corrugated Love Poem 16: Being Seen."

Rob Halpern lives between San Francisco and Ypsilanti, Michigan, where he teaches at Eastern Michigan University and Huron Valley Women's Prison.

WEAK LINK was printed in an edition of
500 copies at Thomson-Shore, Inc.
Text and cover design and typesetting by Derek Fenner
using the old-style serif typeface Garamond.

Atelos was founded in 1995 as a project of Hips Road and is devoted to publishing, under the sign of poetry, writing that challenges conventional, limiting definitions of poetry. All the works published as part of the Atelos project are commissioned specifically for it, and each is involved in some way with crossing traditional genre boundaries, including, for example, those that would separate theory from practice, poetry from prose, essay from drama, the visual image from the verbal, the literary from the non-literary, and so forth. The Atelos project when complete will consist of 50 volumes.

The project directors and editors are Lyn Hejinian and Travis Ortiz. The director for design, cover production, and text production is Derek Fenner.

Atelos (current volumes):

1. The Literal World, by Jean Day
2. Bad History, by Barrett Watten
3. True, by Rae Armantrout
4. Pamela: A Novel, by Pamela Lu
5. Cable Factory 20, by Lytle Shaw
6. R-hu, by Leslie Scalapino
7. Verisimilitude, by Hung Q. Tu
8. Alien Tatters, by Clark Coolidge
9. Forthcoming, by Jalal Toufic
10. Gardener of Stars, by Carla Harryman
11. lighthouse, by M. Mara-Ann
12. Some Vague Wife, by Kathy Lou Schultz
13. The Crave, by Kit Robinson
14. Fashionable Noise, by Brian Kim Stefans
15. Platform, by Rodrigo Toscano
16. Tis of Thee, by Fanny Howe
17 Poetical Dictionary, by Lohren Green
18. BlipSoak01, by Tan Lin
19. The Up and Up, by Ted Greenwald
20. Noh Business, by Murray Edmond

21. Open Clothes, by Steve Benson
22. Occupational Treatment, by Taylor Brady
23. City Eclogue, by Ed Roberson
24. Ultravioleta, by Laura Moriarty
25. Negativity, by Jocelyn Saidenberg
26. The Transformation, by Juliana Spahr
27. To the Cognoscenti, by Tom Mandel
28. Parse, by Craig Dworkin
29. The PoPedology of an Ambient Language, by Edwin Torres
30. The Route, by Patrick Durgin and Jen Hofer
31. To After That (TOAF), by Renee Gladman
32. Last Ditch, by Erik J.M. Schneider
33. Howell, by Tyrone Williams
34. PreDictionary, by Mikhail Epstein
35. Journey to the Sun, by Brent Cunningham
36. Notched Sunsets, by Tim Wood
37. The Coffin Nail Blues, by Ted Pearson
38. Merry Hell, by Sara Larsen
39. The bright red horse—and the blue—Poems , by Katy Lederer
40. The Republic of Exit 43, by Jennifer Scappettone
41. Yaviza, by Roberto Harrison

Distributed by:

Small Press Distribution
1341 Seventh Street
Berkeley, California
94710-1403

Atelos
P O Box 5814
Berkeley, California
94705-0814

to order from SPD call 510-524-1668 or toll-free 800-869-7553
fax orders to: 510-524-0852
order via e-mail at: orders@spdbooks.org
order online from: www.spdbooks.org